WRITING WITH A PURPOSE

NARRATIVE WRITING

—Writing to Tell a Story—

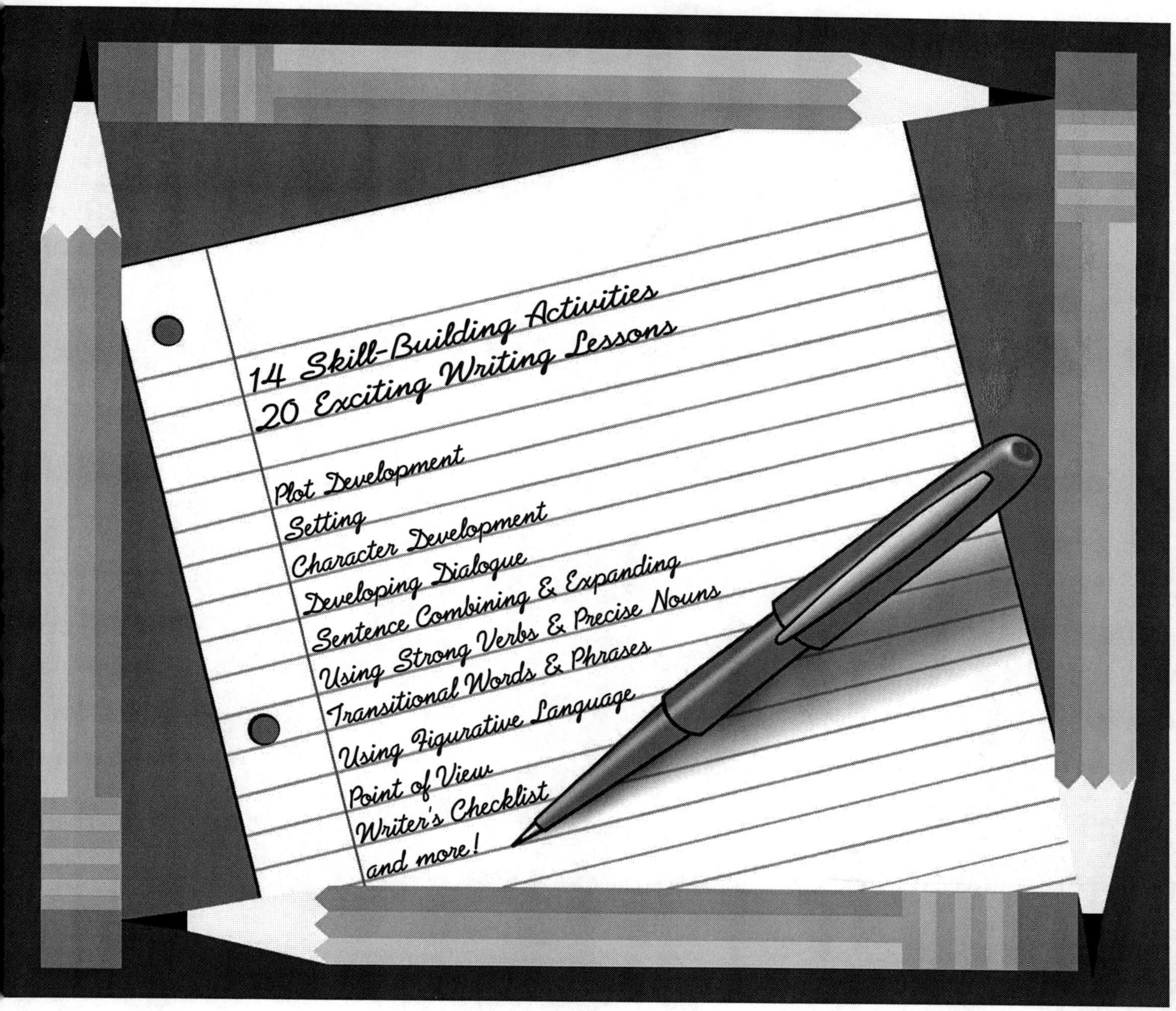

14 Skill-Building Activities
20 Exciting Writing Lessons

Plot Development
Setting
Character Development
Developing Dialogue
Sentence Combining & Expanding
Using Strong Verbs & Precise Nouns
Transitional Words & Phrases
Using Figurative Language
Point of View
Writer's Checklist
and more!

Written by Barbara Doherty and Charlotte Jaffe
Illustrated by Karen Birchak and Koryn Agnello

ISBN 1-56644-097-1 (10-digit)
978-1-56644-097-4 (13-digit)

Printed in the U.S.A.

Table of Contents

TO THE TEACHER 5
REVIEW OF BASIC COMPOSITION SKILLS 6

SKILL-BUILDING ACTIVITIES 7–23
- Let's Narrate 7
- Sentence Combining 8
- Precise Nouns 9
- Strong Verbs 10
- Transitional Words and Phrases 11
- Figurative Language 12
- Time Order and Position Order 13
- Expanding Sentences Using Adjectives, Adverbs, and Prepositions 14
- Plot 15
- Point of View 16
- Setting 17
- Character Development 18
- Developing Dialogue 19
- Mood 20
- Narrative Writing Form 21
- Writer's Checklist 22
- Editorial Symbols 23

NARRATIVE-WRITING LESSONS 24–63
- Lesson 1: On the Job 24–25
- Lesson 2: Create a Myth 26–27
- Lesson 3: The Perfect Day 28–29
- Lesson 4: Dear Diary 30–31
- Lesson 5: Reach for the Stars 32–33
- Lesson 6: You Are There 34–35
- Lesson 7: Proverb Project 36–37
- Lesson 8: Survival Play 38–39
- Lesson 9: Science Fiction 40–41
- Lesson 10: All about Me 42–43
- Lesson 11: A Disappointment 44–45
- Lesson 12: Headliners 46–47
- Lesson 13: Fable Fun 48–49
- Lesson 14: For the Very First Time 50–51
- Lesson 15: Narrative Poetry 52–53
- Lesson 16: A Key Person in My Life 54–55
- Lesson 17: Tell a Tall Tale 56–57
- Lesson 18: Time of Your Life 58–59
- Lesson 19: The Story Behind the Picture 60–61
- Lesson 20: Holiday Memories 62–63

ADDITIONAL TOPIC IDEAS 64

To the Teacher

It is important for children to develop excellent skills in narrative writing. The first part of the book teaches about narrative writing, reviews important composition skills, and provides opportunities for youngsters to practice those skills. Also included are a Writer's Checklist and an Editorial Symbols sheet.

The second part of the book comprises twenty writing lessons. By completing the easy-to-follow activities, students will quickly learn to write a variety of narrative stories and essays. Each two-page lesson is divided into three steps: Pre-Writing, Composing, and Revising. There is also a For-More-Fun activity for each lesson. It provides an opportunity for students to think creatively and to share their writing with their classmates and others. A list of additional topics for narrative writing is also provided.

TEACHING TIPS

- Model a personal narrative by telling your students about one of your own experiences or memories.

- Decide how long you would like each writing product to be and provide guidelines for your students before they begin each lesson.

- Allow enough time for students to write ideas in the Prewriting section; instruct them to use short phrases for this step. In the Compose section, students will develop the phrases into longer, more fluent sentences.

- Encourage your students to work together in a positive way to revise their writing. Assign writing partners before beginning each writing activity. After using the Writer's Checklist, student writing partners can add personal comments. Some sample comments follow:

  This section of writing can be improved by adding or changing…
  What I liked about your narrative writing is…

- Review the list of editorial symbols. Explain their use.

Review of Basic Composition Skills

SENTENCES:
A sentence is a group of words that expresses a complete thought. All sentences start with a capital letter and end with some form of punctuation.

Declarative Sentence: A declarative sentence makes a statement. It ends with a period.
EXAMPLE: I went sledding down a big hill.

Interrogative Sentence: An interrogative sentence asks a question. It ends with a question mark.
EXAMPLE: Will it rain tomorrow?

Exclamatory Sentence: An exclamatory sentence makes a forceful statement. It ends with an exclamation point.
EXAMPLE: Our team won the game!

Imperative Sentence: An imperative sentence gives a command. It ends with a period or an exclamation point.
EXAMPLE: Please bring me the book. Watch out!

Compound Sentences:
To make your writing more interesting, use sentences of different lengths. You can combine two short sentences into a compound sentence. A compound sentence contains two or more simple sentences that are joined by a conjunction. A comma is usually used before the conjunction in a compound sentence.
EXAMPLE: The dinner was delicious. I ate too much.
The dinner was delicious, but I ate too much.

TRANSITIONAL WORDS AND PHRASES:
Words that connect sentences or paragraphs are called transitional words. They include time-order words, space-order words, and words that help to clarify.

Time-Order Words: first, next, last
Space-Order Words: beneath, near, above
Words that Clarify: for instance, however, therefore

CAPITALIZATION RULES:
Capitalize the first word of every sentence.
Capitalize the names of holidays.
Capitalize proper nouns.
Capitalize the names of months and days.
Capitalize the pronoun *I.*
Capitalize the first word of a direct quotation.
Capitalize the first word in the greeting and closing of a letter.
Capitalize the first and every important word in a title.
Capitalize titles or abbreviations with a person's name.

Let's Narrate

A **narrative** is a type of writing that tells a **fiction** or **nonfiction** story. The events of the story are usually described in the order in which they happened. Time-order words are often used to help the story flow properly. Narrative writing has the following components: **setting** (time and place), **characters** (people in the story), and **plot** (story action). A **personal narrative** is told from the first-person point of view. It tells about an event that involves the writer. Types of narrative writing include autobiography, biography, ballad, diary entry, fable, fantasy, journal, log, memory story, myth, and personal experience.

Read the following example of narrative writing. Then answer the questions.

Summer days are usually meant for leisure. Enjoying a cool lemonade, swimming in a refreshing pool, or relaxing with friends on a sun-baked beach are my ideas of summer fun. However, on a hot August afternoon last summer, my father's thoughts were somewhat different. The sun porch badly needed a new coat of fresh yellow paint, and my father insisted that I was just the person to remedy the situation. I agreed and immediately started to paint.

After just one hour, however, the phone rang. It was Lori. I just had to take a break and talk to her. After all, she was my best friend! Then Katie stopped by to tell me about her great vacation. It would have been rude not to listen! When she finally left, my dad walked into the room to inspect my work.

"Hurry up, Jennifer! Why is it taking you so long to paint just one wall?" he questioned in an accusing tone.

"I'm doing my best, Dad!" I responded quickly. "I'll be done soon."

I was just getting back to work when Max, our curious poodle, ran into the room, knocking over the pail of paint and then decorating the rug with yellow pawprints. What a mess! What a cleanup job!

So here I am, late in the afternoon, painting the porch on a day that should have been filled with summer fun. Next time my father asks me to do a job like this, I think I'll ask if it could be done at a different time of year.

1. Which words indicate proper time sequence?

____

2. In what way was dialogue used to enhance the story?

____

3. How was humor used in this personal narrative?

____

Sentence Combining

In order to make your writing more interesting and readable, try to combine short, choppy sentences into one longer, smoother sentence. In this way, you will eliminate repeated words.

EXAMPLE: Jake is a dog. Jake is a small dog. Jake is a gray dog.
Jake is a small, gray dog.

You can also combine two or more simple sentences into a longer, compound sentence. Don't forget to add a comma before the conjunction when you have a compound subject!

EXAMPLE: Does Samantha like chocolate ice cream? Does she prefer vanilla?
Does Samantha like chocolate ice cream, or does she prefer vanilla?

Combine Them!

Combine each of the following short sentences into one new, more effective one.

1. The band lined up. The band marched down the field.

____

2. We planned an outdoor party. It started to rain.

____

3. Ben threw the ball. I caught it.

____

4. The plane landed on the runway. The plane was large. The plane was silver.

____

5. Kyle wanted to swim. The pool was closed.

____

6. Brooke tied the gift box with a ribbon. The ribbon was thin. The ribbon was red.

____

7. Will you bring your lunch? Will you buy a lunch platter?

____

8. Ryan played the piano. The audience applauded.

____

Writing Activity

Use sentence combining to write a paragraph describing how you achieved a goal.

____

____

____

____

____

____

Precise Nouns

Nouns provide important information. They are used to name persons, things, and ideas. Use **specific nouns** to make your writing clearer and more exact.

EXAMPLE: In order to repair the machine, I will need tools.
In order to repair the dishwasher, I will need pliers, a wrench, and some screws.

Replace Them!

Replace the underlined noun in the sentence with a more precise one. You may make other changes as necessary.

1. The worker has just left the building for the day.

____

2. My friend recently moved to a different city.

____

3. The store shelves were crowded with sports equipment.

____

4. Lori bought new jewelry to wear to the special occasion.

____

5. I see a boat sailing down the waterway.

____

6. Our relative bought us an animal to keep as a house pet.

____

7. We'll celebrate the holiday with our favorite food.

____

8. Musical instruments were loaned to the fifth-grade students.

____

Writing Activity

Think of a precise noun for each of the following nouns and use them in sentences about springtime.

Tree: ____

Bird: ____

Place: ____

Flower: ____

Insect: ____

Weather: ____

Strong Verbs

Verbs have power. They express action or a state of being. Your choice of verbs in a sentence can make a big difference in your writing. Read the sentences below. What differences can you notice?

Last night Maria **ate** her dinner.
Last night Maria **devoured** her dinner.
Last night Maria **nibbled** her dinner.

The verb in the second sentence makes it clear that Maria was very hungry last night. The verb in the third example tells us that Maria was not very hungry at all. It is important to use **exact verbs** in your writing.

Many verbs are overused. Try to make your sentences more lively and interesting by using vivid verbs. Try not to rely on common verbs such as *say, look,* or *walk.* Read the sentences below. What difference can you notice?

The woman **looked** at the mischievous little girl.
The woman **glared** at the mischievous little girl.

The verb in the second example tells us that the woman was angry at the little girl.

Make Them Strong

Write two strong verbs for each common verb listed on the left.

1. Like ____________________ ____________________
2. Make ____________________ ____________________
3. Sit ____________________ ____________________
4. Talk ____________________ ____________________
5. Call ____________________ ____________________
6. Want ____________________ ____________________
7. See ____________________ ____________________
8. Play ____________________ ____________________

Writing Activity

Locate newspaper headlines from articles written for your local newspaper. Change the verbs in the headlines. Write a story that the new headline describes.

Transitional Words and Phrases That Help to Clarify

Transitional words and phrases are useful in joining related phrases, sentences, paragraphs, and ideas together. They make the jump from one thought to another much smoother. Included are time-order words and phrases, position-order words and phrases, and words and phrases that help clarify what the writer or speaker is telling us. In this exercise you will use transitional words and phrases that help clarify. Some help to compare and contrast, some help to summarize, and some help us to understand cause and effect.

EXAMPLE: My little brother started to cry **because** he lost his toy.
"Because" is a transitional word. It helps us understand why the speaker or writer's little brother began to cry.

Words and Phrases that Help to Clarify

additionally	all in all	although	as a result
as soon as	because	but	even though
finally	for example	for this reason	however
in conclusion	in fact	in other words	in summary
in the end	lastly	like	likewise
nevertheless	similarly	since	therefore

Connect Them

Use transitional words and phrases to connect the following sentences and to clarify the meaning. You may choose from the list above or use others of your own choice.

1. Janet returned to the team. We won more games.

____

2. Blue is my favorite color. I like red, too.

____

3. We were tired. We had to go home.

____

4. I saw my cousin from out of state. I recognized her.

____

5. I like to stay up late. I had to go to bed.

____

Writing Activity

Construct six pairs of sentences. Exchange them with a few of your classmates. Have them connect the pairs of sentences with transitional words and phrases. Which words were used? How did the different words change the meanings of the sentences? Were any transitional words or phrases used which were not on the list above?

Figurative Language

Authors and poets often use literary devices called **figures of speech** to make their writing more colorful. In a figure of speech, words and phrases have meanings that are different from their usual ones. Here are some types of figurative language.

SIMILES
A simile makes a comparison of two dissimilar things using words such as *like* or *as.*

EXAMPLE: The lights of the city looked like flickering fireflies.

METAPHORS
A metaphor compares two dissimilar things without using words such as *like* or *as.* It makes the comparison by saying something *is* something else.

EXAMPLE: The falling raindrops were shiny jewels in a carpet of grass.

PERSONIFICATION
In personification inanimate objects or abstract ideas are given human qualities.

EXAMPLE: The leaves danced in the wind.

Identify the Figure of Speech

Read the following sentences. Tell if each contains a simile, a metaphor, or a personification.

1. The sun smiled down on us. ____________________
2. Her eyes lit up like the lights on a Christmas tree. ____________________
3. The setting sun was a red balloon in the evening sky. ____________________

Writing Activity

Use each phrase in a sentence to create your own simile, metaphor, or personification.

1. Loud thunder ____
2. The old elm tree ____
3. Flowers in my garden ____
4. Falling leaves ____
5. The blue sea ____
6. Children's laughter ____

Time Order and Position Order

Time order is the order in which things happen in time. In your writing, start at the beginning and give details in the order in which they occur. Here are some time-order words and phrases to help you.

first	**second**	**next**	**after**	**last**	**now**	**later**
before	**until**	**meanwhile**	**at last**	**immediately**	**after a while**	
as soon as	**all of a sudden**	**afterwards**	**finally**	**during**		

Position-order, or space-order, words and phrases help to organize descriptive details in your writing. Organize details from top to bottom, front to back, near to far, left to right, or the reverse. Here are some position-order words and phrases to help you.

near	**beneath**	**in front of**	**next**	**in**	**nearby**	**on**
between	**in back of**	**around**	**on top of**	**to the left**		
to the right	**underneath**	**inside**	**above**			

Put Them in Order

Put the following sentences in the correct time order.

_____ Then the ski instructor showed him how to balance on skis.

_____ One day Alex decided to learn to ski.

_____ He soon learned the elements of skiing.

_____ Finally, Alex was able to ski down the hill alone.

_____ At first, Alex was scared when he stood at the top of the hill.

In what order would you arrange the details that you would use to describe the following items? Choose from top to bottom, left to right, near to far, front to back, or the reverse.

1. Toys on a shelf ______________________________
2. Chapters in a book ______________________________
3. Words in a sentence ______________________________
4. A stack of magazines ______________________________
5. Rows of desks in a classroom ______________________________

Writing Activity

1. Think about a typical day in your life. Write about it using correct time order.
2. Describe your bedroom. Use space-order words to organize the details of your bedroom.

Expanding Sentences Using Adjectives, Adverbs, and Prepositions

Adjectives are used to describe nouns and pronouns. They can add colorful details and information to your writing. The second sentence provides a better word picture.

The streets were crowded with traffic.
The narrow streets were crowded with noisy traffic.

What other adjectives could be used to describe the noun *streets* in order to change the scene?

______________________ ______________________ ______________________

What other adjectives could be used to describe the noun *traffic* in order to change the scene?

______________________ ______________________ ______________________

Adverbs are used to modify, or qualify the meaning of, verbs, adjectives, and other adverbs. They tell how, when, where, and to what extent. The correct use of adverbs can improve your writing. The second sentence provides a better word picture.

The airplane landed after a long flight.
The airplane landed safely after an extremely long flight.

What other adverbs could be used to modify the verb *landed* in order to change the scene?

______________________ ______________________ ______________________

What other adverbs could be used to modify the adjective *long* in order to change the scene?

______________________ ______________________ ______________________

Prepositions relate words to other words in a sentence. Prepositional phrases can be used to tell how, when, or where. The second sentence provides a better word picture.

The wind blew.
During the night the wind blew through my open window.

What other prepositional phrases could be used in order to change the scene?

______________________ ______________________ ______________________

______________________ ______________________ ______________________

Writing Activity

Create parts-of-speech poetry. Choose adjectives, adverbs, or prepositions to enhance a four-line poem. First write the poem without the added parts of speech. Then rewrite it with the parts of speech included. Share your poem orally with your classmates.

Plot

The **plot** of a narrative is the sequence of events that tells what happens in the story. A plot is usually divided into the following parts:

Beginning or Introduction: The **setting** and some of the **characters** are described. The plot begins.

Middle: The main character faces a **conflict** or problem in this part of the story. The story builds in action and excitement towards the **climax,** or turning point.

Ending: The action of the plot winds down. The main character or characters **resolve the problem.**

Guess the Story

Try to guess the well-known story that is suggested in the plot below.

1. A beautiful young woman is lost in the woods.
2. Seven short men find the young woman and offer her shelter.
3. Her jealous, evil stepmother tricks the young woman into eating a poisoned fruit.
4. The young woman is rescued by a handsome prince.

The story is ____.

Writing Activity

Write a plot outline for a story that you know. The following is a plot outline for *Goldilocks and the Three Bears.*

Beginning or Introduction: The setting is a cottage near the woods.
We meet Mama Bear, Papa Bear, and Baby Bear.

Middle: Goldilocks enters the Bears' home. She eats porridge, destroys furniture, and sleeps in a bed.
When the Bears arrive home, Goldilocks runs away.

Ending: The Bears live happily ever after.

PLOT OUTLINE FOR ________________________

Beginning:

Middle:

Ending:

Point of View

In narrative writing **point of view** refers to the voice that is telling the story. Some stories have a **first-person narrator**, who describes the action and refers to himself or herself as "I." Other stories have a **third-person narrator**. When there is a third-person point of view, the narrator is not a character in the story; he or she describes the action as an observer.

EXAMPLES:
First-Person Narrator: I cannot find the key to my door.
Third-Person Narrator: She cannot find the key to her door.

Change the Point of View

The sentences below are written in the third-person point of view. Rewrite them so that they are in the first-person point of view by changing the underlined words. Make any other necessary changes.

1. <u>Their</u> new dog has given <u>them</u> lots of pleasure.
2. <u>Bob</u> walked slowly back to <u>his</u> house.
3. <u>She</u> helps <u>her</u> brother with his homework.
4. <u>He</u> likes to ride <u>his</u> bike to school.
5. <u>Joan</u> and <u>the writer</u> presented a project to t<u>heir</u> classmates.

Writing Activity

Think of something interesting that you did or experienced recently at home, at school, or at play. Describe it first from your point of view using first-person narration. Then describe it from a friend's or a relative's point of view using third-person narration.

____

____

____

____

____

____

____

____

____

____

____

____

Setting

The **setting** of a narrative is the **time and place** of the story action. The story setting is important because it directly affects the plot. Where will your story take place? Will it take place in the past, in the present, or in the world of the future? Is the time setting late at night or during the daylight? Does the setting change during the story?

Sometimes the author directly states the setting as in the following example:

In 1995 I spent a special summer with my cousins in a small Wisconsin town.

Sometimes the author informs the readers about the setting of the story through details that hint at the time and location as in the following example:

The Statue of Liberty beamed in the bright sunlight as our ship approached the pier.

Writing Activity

Create a modern setting for a well-known story that is set long ago. Rewrite a portion of the story in the new setting. How has the new setting influenced the plot and character development? Fairy tales, historical-fiction stories, and Shakespearean plays are some possibilities.

Character Development

Review the plot of the narrative that you plan to write and decide what characters are needed to tell your story. Think about how each character might look, think, feel, act, and speak. Use the form to help you develop those characters.

CHARACTER 1

Name and Age: ____________________

Physical Appearance: ____________________

Personality Traits: ____________________

Typical Quote: ____________________

CHARACTER 2

Name and Age: ____________________

Physical Appearance: ____________________

Personality Traits: ____________________

Typical Quote: ____________________

CHARACTER 3

Name and Age: ____________________

Physical Appearance: ____________________

Personality Traits: ____________________

Typical Quote: ____________________

CHARACTER 4

Name and Age: ____________________

Physical Appearance: ____________________

Personality Traits: ____________________

Typical Quote: ____________________

Writing Activity

Write the beginning of your story plot in the space below using some or all of the characters you have developed.

____

____

____

____

____

____

____

____

Developing Dialogue

When you include a character's exact words in your writing, you are using **dialogue.** Dialogue is written conversation. This technique helps the characters in your story come alive through the words they speak. Each speaker's exact words are punctuated and set apart with quotation marks.

RULES TO REMEMBER

Use a comma to separate the speaker from the direct quotation. Do not add a comma if the quotation ends with a question mark or an exclamation point.

Put the end punctuation inside the quotation marks.

Begin the first word of the quotation with a capital letter.

Start each new speaker's words on a different line.

EXAMPLE:

Juan said, "I'd like to start a hobby."
"Why don't you collect stamps?" asked Tim.

INTERRUPTED QUOTATIONS

If the quotation is one sentence, begin and end the first part with quotation marks and add commas to separate the speaker from the quotation. Use correct end punctuation. If the divided quotation is written as two sentences, use a period (or other end punctuation) to separate the sentences and begin each part with quotation marks and capital letters.

EXAMPLES:

"Did you remember," asked Mom, "to pack your lunch?"
"It's raining now," said Mrs. Andrews. "We'll have to postpone the school picnic."

Writing Activity

Choose one of the following character pairs and create a dialogue between them. Use some interrupted quotations in your dialogue.

1. Two Friends   2. Teacher and Parent   3. Coach and Player

____

____

____

____

____

____

____

____

Mood

Mood is the feeling or effect that is created by the author's words. Settings, actions, characterizations, and descriptions can all be written to convey certain moods. Read the following selections from familiar novels and think about how these passages make you feel.

1. *Hatchet,* by Gary Paulson
" At first he thought it was a growl. In the still of the darkness of the shelter in the middle of the night, his eyes came open and he was awake."

____

2. *James and the Giant Peach,* by Roald Dahl
" 'Look at me, look at me!" shouted the Centipede excitedly. "It's washed me clean! The paint's all gone! I can move again!' "

____

3. *Dear Mr. Henshaw,* by Beverly Cleary
" 'I wish somebody would ask me over sometime. After school I stay around kicking a soccer ball with some of the other kids so they won't think I am stuck up or something, but nobody asks me over.' "

____

4. *Walk Two Moons,* by Sharon Creech
"The reason Gramps cried when he carried Gram into the house was that there, in the center of the bedroom, stood his own parents' bed—the bed that Gramps and each of his brothers had been born in, the bed his parents always slept in."

____

Writing Activity

Write a sentence to convey each of the following moods. Use words and phrases that fit the mood.

Happiness

____

Fear

____

Anger

____

Astonishment

____

Narrative Writing Forms

Narrative writing can be divided into two classifications: **fiction** and **nonfiction.** **Fiction** is an imaginative work of literature. It is a made-up story about real or imaginary people or events. **Non-fiction** is literature that tells a true story about real people and events.

STORY FORM FOR FICTION OR NONFICTION NARRATIVE WRITING

BEGINNING

Describe the setting time and place.

Example: City Swim Center in the summer of 1999.

Give important background information.

Example: My name is Mike. I was ten years old, and this was my first major swim meet.

Start to tell what happened.

Example: We all lined up at the edge of the pool.

MIDDLE

Introduce and describe other people involved in the narrative.

Example: Joe, the swimming coach, was friendly but strict. Ed, another member of the team, was jealous of me. Scott, also on the team, was a good friend.

Discuss the conflict or problem that arises.

Example: Just as I was about to enter the pool, I tripped over an object.

Continue the action of the story.

Example: Tripping gave me a late start, and my leg hurt.

Build toward a climax.

Example: With my leg in pain, I swam with my best effort. Ed won the competition. I managed to come in second.

CONCLUSION

Wind down the action of the plot and explain how the conflict or problem is resolved.

Example: Scott told the coach that he witnessed Ed putting the object by the pool. Ed admitted his guilt, and Coach Joe disqualified him from the team. I won the race.

Writer's Checklist

This checklist provides some useful guidelines to remember when you write. Use it both for self-evaluation and for evaluation of your peers.

___ 1. Did you compose a good opening sentence that will catch the attention of the reader?

___ 2. Do you have a single focus in your writing? Did you stick to one topic?

___ 3. Is your writing organized? Does it progress logically from beginning to end? Is it clearly written and easy to follow?

___ 4. Did you use details in your writing that clarify and support the main topic?

___ 5. If you are writing non-fiction, did you make sure your writing is accurate?

___ 6. Did you check your work for spelling, punctuation, and grammar errors?

___ 7. Did you use sentence variety in your writing? Are your sentences of varied lengths? Did you start your sentences with different words?

___ 8. Did you use word variety in your writing? Check to see that you did not use the same word over and over.

___ 9. Did you use vivid vocabulary in your writing? Are your words interesting and colorful?

___ 10. If you used figures of speech, were they appropriate?

___ 11. Did you try the use of transitional words and phrases between paragraphs to make your writing easier to follow and understand?

___ 12. Did you use a good closing sentence? Does it sum up your writing in an effective way?

___ 13. Did you check your first draft carefully before attempting to revise and rewrite your work?

___ 14. Did you type your work or write it in a legible manner? Will people be able to read your work easily?

Writing Partner's Personal Comments:

____

____

____

____

____

Editorial Symbols

The following editorial symbols are some common symbols used in proofreading and editing. A caret or a line is used within the text to show where the correction should be made. A circle around instructions in the margin means not to include what's circled in the text.

IN MARGIN	MEANING	IN TEXT
(delete mark)	delete or take out	Take it ~~it~~ out.
⁀	close up; no space	The book is in the book bag.
father	replace	Joe visited his ~~mother~~.
#	insert space	Shewent to the store.
a	insert a letter, punctuation, or word	Anne, give the tall man book.
(ital)	set in italics	I just read Little Women.
(bf)	set in bold	Editorial Marks
(cap)	capitalize	joan and I went to the movies.
(lc)	lower case	The River was very high.
⊙	insert period	I asked her to come
^,	insert comma	She had a book a poster, and a magazine.
^;	insert semicolon	I went to the class so did Sue.
“ / ”	insert quotation marks	Go to bed, said Mrs. Jones.
’	insert apostrophe	Id like to go now.
(tr)	transpose words	The boy tall can reach the high shelf.
(tr)	transpose lines	Bring it here. Find the box.
¶	make new paragraph	¶Dogs are very useful to humans. They have been trained as hunters. Some are used for security. Others are work animals, pulling carts and sleds. Many dogs help people with handicaps maintain their independence. Dogs are very good companions.
no ¶	no new paragraph	Dogs are very useful to humans. They have been trained as hunters. Some are used for security. Others are work animals, pulling carts and sleds. Many dogs help people with handicaps maintain their independence. Dogs are very good companions.

On the Job

TOPIC

Some jobs can be difficult and unrewarding. In a short essay, tell about a time when you had to do a job or task that you did not like.

THINK ABOUT IT

What kind of job did you attempt to do? Where did you do the work? How did you get the job? What other people were part of the job experience? What happened that made it difficult to complete the job? How did you feel as you were working on the job? What did you learn from your job experience?

GET ORGANIZED

Plan your narrative writing. Start out with an effective opening sentence and describe the narrative events in the order that they happened. Add details to help the reader experience the story. Include dialogue to make the characters in your writing come to life. Write a strong ending to your essay. Use the thought webs on this page to record your ideas for your narrative writing.

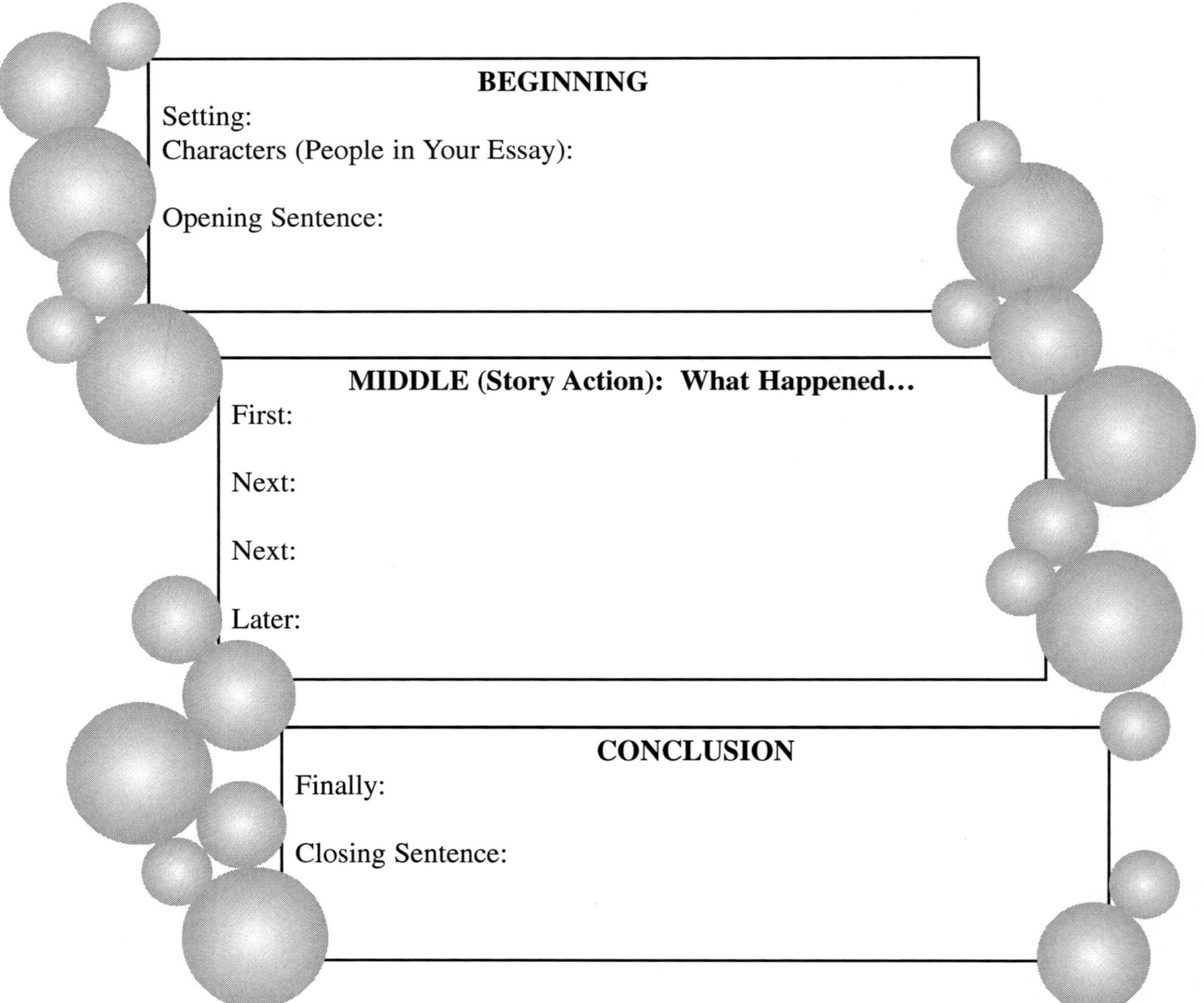

BEGINNING

Setting:

Characters (People in Your Essay):

Opening Sentence:

MIDDLE (Story Action): What Happened…

First:

Next:

Next:

Later:

CONCLUSION

Finally:

Closing Sentence:

On the Job

COMPOSE

Remember to write your narrative essay with a clear beginning, middle, and conclusion. Create interesting and expressive opening and closing sentences and strive for sentence and word variety. Don't forget to stay on topic as you write! Use details and dialogue to help your essay develop fully. Relate the story events in the order that they occurred. Refer to your writing ideas from the pre-writing section to get started.

REVISE

Edit your essay by using the Writer's Checklist and the Editorial Symbols sheets. Then exchange papers with your pre-assigned writing partner. Each of you will use the same sheets to offer suggestions for improvement to the other. Now you are ready to rewrite your work in good form on another paper. Share the story with the whole class.

JUST-FOR-FUN ACTIVITY

Write a how-to magazine article based on the job you described. Some examples follow: "How to Babysit for a Difficult Child," "Cleaning a Messy Bedroom," and "Shortcuts to Lawn Care." Share your articles with your classmates and assemble them into a magazine format. Create a name and cover for your class how-to magazine.

Create a Myth

TOPIC

Scientists have developed reasons and theories that solve the mystery of everyday occurrences. The following are some examples: What causes a rainbow to appear? Why do birds migrate? Why is the sea salty? Choose one scientific question and create a myth to explain the phenomenon.

THINK ABOUT IT

What is the scientific question? How did the event look, sound, smell, or feel? In your myth, who or what might have caused it to occur? Where did it happen? What were the reasons that it happened? Why did it continue to occur? What other characters were involved in the myth? What problems were associated with it? How were these problems solved?

GET ORGANIZED

Plan your myth. Start out with an effective opening sentence and describe the narrative events in the order that they happened. Add details to help the reader experience the story. Include dialogue to make the characters in your writing come to life. Write a strong ending to your myth. Use the thought webs on this page to record your ideas for your myth.

BEGINNING

Setting:

Characters:

Opening Sentence:

MIDDLE (Story Action): What Happened…

First:

Next:

Next:

Later:

CONCLUSION

Finally:

Closing Sentence:

Create a Myth

COMPOSE

Remember to write your myth with a clear beginning, middle, and conclusion. Create interesting and expressive opening and closing sentences and strive for sentence and word variety. Don't forget to stay on topic as you write! Use details and dialogue to help you develop your myth more fully. Relate the story events in the order that they occurred. Refer to your writing ideas from the pre-writing section to get started.

REVISE

Edit your myth by using the Writer's Checklist and the Editorial Symbols sheets. Then exchange papers with your pre-assigned writing partner. Each of you will use the same sheets to offer suggestions for improvement to the other. Now you are ready to rewrite your work in good form on another paper. Share the story with the whole class.

FOR MORE FUN

Create a mobile that represents characters and events in your myth. Read the myth to a group of younger students. Share the mobile with them to enhance the story.

The Perfect Day

TOPIC

Recall a special day in your life that you really enjoyed. On this day, everything turned out better than expected. Perhaps it was a birthday, a holiday, or a noteworthy day at school. Write a story by telling about your perfect day.

THINK ABOUT IT

How did your day start? Where and when did the activity of the day take place? Who else was involved in the day's events? What did you hope to achieve on this day? What happened to make this a perfect day for you? How did you feel when the day was over?

GET ORGANIZED

Plan your narrative writing. Start out with an effective opening sentence and describe the narrative events in the order that they happened. Add details to help the reader experience the story. Include dialogue to make the characters in your writing come to life. Write a strong ending to your story. Use the thought webs on this page to record your ideas for your narrative writing.

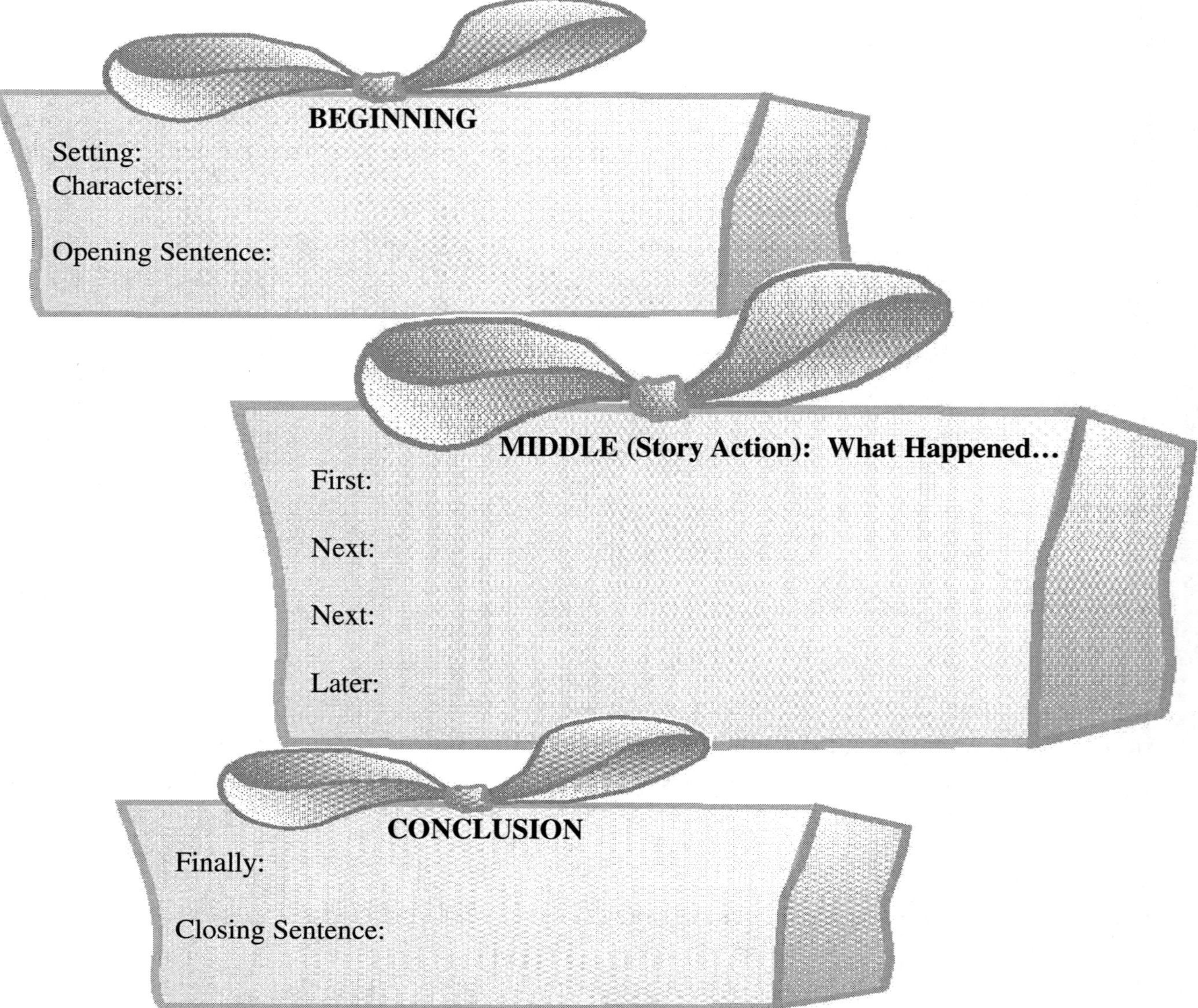

The Perfect Day

COMPOSE

Remember to write your narrative story with a clear beginning, middle, and conclusion. Create interesting and expressive opening and closing sentences and strive for sentence and word variety. Don't forget to stay on topic as you write! Use details and dialogue to help your story develop fully. Relate the story events in the order that they occurred. Refer to your writing ideas from the pre-writing section to get started.

REVISE

Edit your story by using the Writer's Checklist and the Editorial Symbols sheets. Then exchange papers with your pre-assigned writing partner. Each of you will use the same sheets to offer suggestions for improvement to the other. Now you are ready to rewrite your work in good form on another paper. Share the story with the whole class.

FOR MORE FUN

Construct a roller movie that details the events of your perfect day. You will need a cardboard box; wooden or paper dowels; white construction paper; scissors; tape; and markers, crayons, or paints. Draw or paint the scenes on the white paper. Arrange them in logical sequence and secure them together with the tape. Cut out an area of the box to use as a movie screen. Cut holes in the box for the dowels. Insert the dowels in the holes and tape the last picture to the bottom dowel. Roll up the pictures and tape the first picture to the top dowel. Move the dowels to show your movie.

Dear Diary

TOPIC
You are on a fun-filled family vacation. Write an entry in your travel diary detailing a special adventure or happening that you experienced during your vacation days.

THINK ABOUT IT
Where and when did your experience begin? What did you see, hear, and feel as your adventure developed? What other people were part of the action? What problems did you encounter? How were the problems solved? How did your adventure end?

GET ORGANIZED
Plan your narrative writing. Start out with an effective opening sentence and describe the narrative events in the order that they happened. Add details to help the reader experience the story. Include dialogue to make the characters in your diary entry come to life. Write a strong ending to your entry. Use the thought webs on this page to record your ideas for your narrative writing.

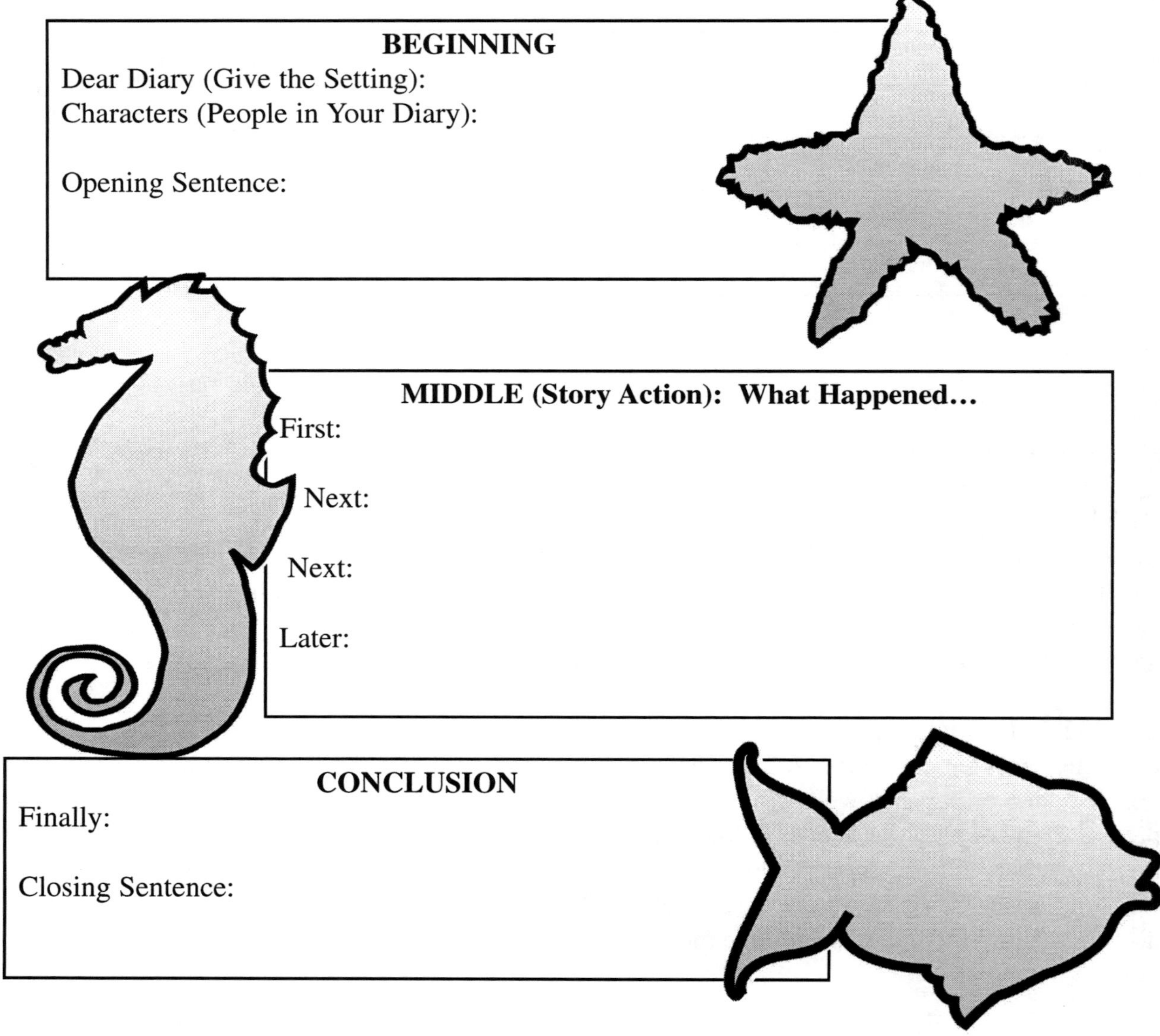

Dear Diary

COMPOSE

Remember to write your diary entry with a clear beginning, middle, and conclusion. Create interesting and expressive opening and closing sentences and strive for sentence and word variety. Don't forget to stay on topic as you write! Use details and dialogue to help you develop your diary entry more fully. Relate the story events in the order that they occurred. Refer to your writing ideas from the pre-writing section to get started.

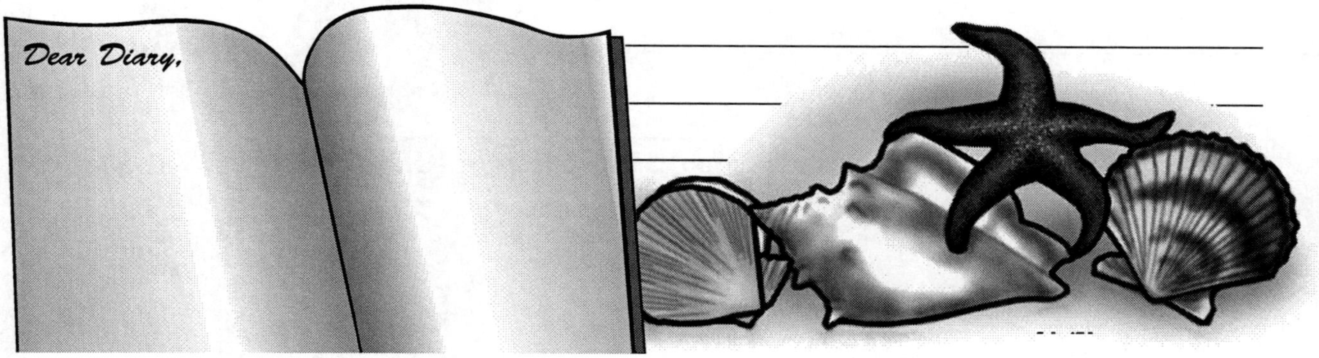

Dear Diary,

REVISE

Edit your narrative writing by using the Writer's Checklist and the Editorial Symbols sheets. Then exchange papers with your pre-assigned writing partner. Each of you will use the same sheets to offer suggestions for improvement to the other. Now you are ready to rewrite your work in good form on another paper. Share the story with the whole class.

FOR MORE FUN

Design and illustrate a travel poster that highlights your family vacation trip. Attach your diary entry to it and display it in the hall or school library.

Reach for the Stars

TOPIC

Have you ever felt proud of yourself because you finally accomplished a difficult feat or reached a long-sought-after goal? Write a narrative essay that details your accomplishment.

THINK ABOUT IT

What was your goal? Why was it important to you? Describe your first plans and efforts to reach the goal. What other people were involved in the endeavor? Did they help or hinder you? What problems did you face in fulfilling the accomplishment? How did you overcome these problems? Where and when did your accomplishment take place? Describe your feelings when you reached your goal.

GET ORGANIZED

Plan your narrative writing. Start out with an effective opening sentence and describe the narrative events in the order that they happened. Add details to help the reader experience the story. Include dialogue to make the characters in your writing come to life. Write a strong ending to your essay. Use the thought webs on this page to record your ideas for your narrative writing.

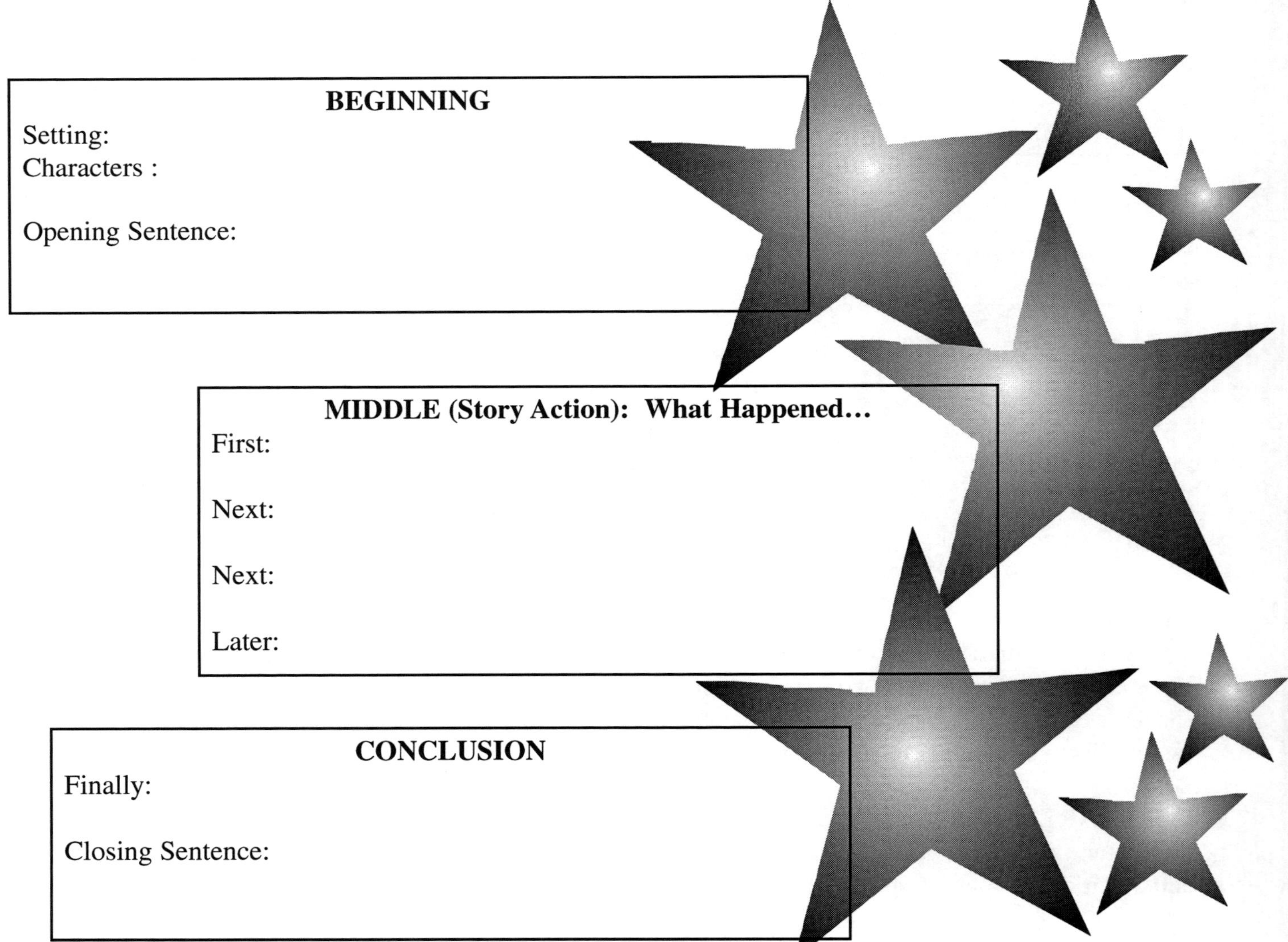

Reach for the Stars

COMPOSE

Remember to write your narrative essay with a clear beginning, middle, and conclusion. Create interesting and expressive opening and closing sentences and strive for sentence and word variety. Don't forget to stay on topic as you write! Use details and dialogue to help your essay develop fully. Relate the story events in the order that they occurred. Refer to your writing ideas from the pre-writing section to get started.

REVISE

Edit your essay by using the Writer's Checklist and the Editorial Symbols sheets. Then exchange papers with your pre-assigned writing partner. Each of you will use the same sheets to offer suggestions for improvement to the other. Now you are ready to rewrite your work in good form on another paper. Share the story with the whole class.

FOR MORE FUN

Create a blue-ribbon award out of construction paper. Draw a picture of your accomplishment on the top part of the ribbon and label it. Attach the essay to the ribbon and display the writing on the class bulletin board.

You Are There

TOPIC

Imagine that you are living in the past and are part of an important historical event. Possible events are Sailing with Christopher Columbus, Helping Harriet Tubman with the Underground Railroad, and Fighting in the Revolutionary War. Write a letter to a friend or relative describing the events surrounding your exciting experience.

THINK ABOUT IT

What year is it? Look around. Where are you? Who is with you? What do you see, hear, feel, or smell? What is happening? In what ways are you involved in the situation? What problems do you and the others face? How will these problems be resolved? Why is this experience such a special one?

GET ORGANIZED

Plan your letter. Start out with an effective opening sentence and describe the narrative events in the order that they happened. Add details to help the reader experience the story. Include dialogue to make the characters in your writing come to life. Write a strong ending to your letter. Use the thought webs on this page to record your ideas for your narrative writing.

BEGINNING

Historical Event:
Setting:
Characters:

Opening Sentence:

MIDDLE (Story Action): What Happened...

First:

Next:

Next:

Later:

CONCLUSION

Finally:

Closing Sentence:

You Are There

COMPOSE

Remember to write your narrative letter with a clear beginning, middle, and conclusion. Create interesting and expressive opening and closing sentences and strive for sentence and word variety. Don't forget to stay on topic as you write! Use details and dialogue to help you develop your letter more fully. Relate the story events in the order that they occurred. Refer to your writing ideas from the pre-writing section to get started.

REVISE

Edit your letter by using the Writer's Checklist and the Editorial Symbols sheets. Then exchange papers with your pre-assigned writing partner. Each of you will use the same sheets to offer suggestions for improvement to the other. Now you are ready to rewrite your work in good form on another paper. Share the story with the whole class.

FOR MORE FUN

Use your letter from history as the outline for a historical skit. Add more dialogue to your writing and develop it into a script. Ask some of your classmates to take the roles of characters in your play. Create simple props and costumes. Perform the historical skit for parents and other classmates.

Proverb Project

TOPIC

Proverbs are famous old sayings that people sometimes use to make a point or to close an argument. Brainstorm and list as many proverbs as you can. Then choose a familiar proverb and write a story using that proverb as the central theme. The following are examples of proverbs: Beauty is in the eyes of the beholder. An apple a day keeps the doctor away. A place for everything, and everything in its place. Too many cooks spoil the broth.

THINK ABOUT IT

Explain the meaning of the proverb you have chosen. How can you use the proverb in a story? What is the setting of your story? Who are the main and supporting characters? What happens to the characters as the plot develops? Do the story characters change their ideas and feelings? How are the story problems resolved? How do the characters carry out the proverb theme?

GET ORGANIZED

Plan your story. Start with an effective opening sentence and describe the narrative events in the order that they happened. Add details to help the reader experience the story. Include dialogue to make the characters in your writing come to life. Write a strong ending to your story. Use the thought webs on this page to record your ideas for your narrative writing.

Proverb Project

COMPOSE

Remember to write your narrative story with a clear beginning, middle, and conclusion. Create interesting and expressive opening and closing sentences and strive for sentence and word variety. Don't forget to stay on topic as you write! Use details and dialogue to help your story develop fully. Relate the story events in the order that they occurred. Refer to your writing ideas from the pre-writing section to get started.

REVISE

Edit your narrative writing by using the Writer's Checklist and the Editorial Symbols sheets. Then exchange papers with your pre-assigned writing partner. Each of you will use the same sheets to offer suggestions for improvement to the other. Now you are ready to rewrite your work in good form on another paper. Share the story with the whole class.

FOR MORE FUN

Create a proverb board game. See how many proverbs you can include in your game. Design information cards and construct markers to move around the board. Write a set of directions. Have a class Game Day and exchange the proverb games.

Survival Play

TOPIC

You have been chosen to write the class play for the annual school Play Day. This year's theme is Survival. Write your play using the proper form for play scripts. Write each character's name with capital letters followed by a colon. Add stage directions in parentheses. For example:

RYAN: (nervously) This ship has become quite rocky.

THINK ABOUT IT

What is the setting of your play? Who are the main and supporting characters? How does your survival story plot begin? What happens to the characters as the play develops? In what ways do the characters face danger? How do they deal with their problems? What is the resolution of the plot? How will you divide your play into acts and scenes?

GET ORGANIZED

Plan your narrative writing. Start out with an effective opening sentence and describe the narrative events in the order that they happened. Add details to help the reader experience the story. Use stage directions to enhance the dialogue of the characters. Write a strong ending to your play. Use the thought webs on this page to record your ideas.

BEGINNING

Setting:

Characters:

Opening Line and Stage Direction:

MIDDLE (Story Action): What Happened...

First:

Next:

Next:

Later:

CONCLUSION

Finally:

Closing Sentence:

Survival Play

COMPOSE

Remember to write your play with a clear beginning, middle, and conclusion. Create interesting and suitable opening and closing lines for your play. Strive for sentence and word variety. Don't forget to stay on topic as you write! Use details and dialogue to help develop the plot of your play more fully. Relate the story events in the order that they occurred. Refer to your writing ideas from the pre-writing section to get started.

REVISE

Edit your play by using the Writer's Checklist and the Editorial Symbols sheets. Then exchange papers with your pre-assigned writing partner. Each of you will use the same sheets to offer suggestions for improvement to the other. Now you are ready to rewrite your work in good form on another paper. Share the story with the whole class.

FOR MORE FUN

Present your survival play in the form of a puppet show. Design puppet characters using paper bags, socks, or other types. Ask classmates to take parts in the play presentation. Add background scenery to enhance the production.

Science Fiction

TOPIC

Enter a science-fiction writing contest! In your story, include several elements that are often found in science-fiction stories, such as robots, time and space travel, space wars, and technology and invention. Good luck in the contest!

THINK ABOUT IT

What is the setting of your story? Who are the main and supporting characters? What problems do the characters have? What happens to them as the plot proceeds? What makes the story science fiction?

GET ORGANIZED

Plan your science-fiction writing. Start out with an effective opening sentence and describe the narrative events in the order that they happened. Add details to help the reader experience the story. Include dialogue to make the characters in your writing come to life. Write a strong ending to your narrative account. Use the thought webs on this page to record your ideas for your science-fiction story.

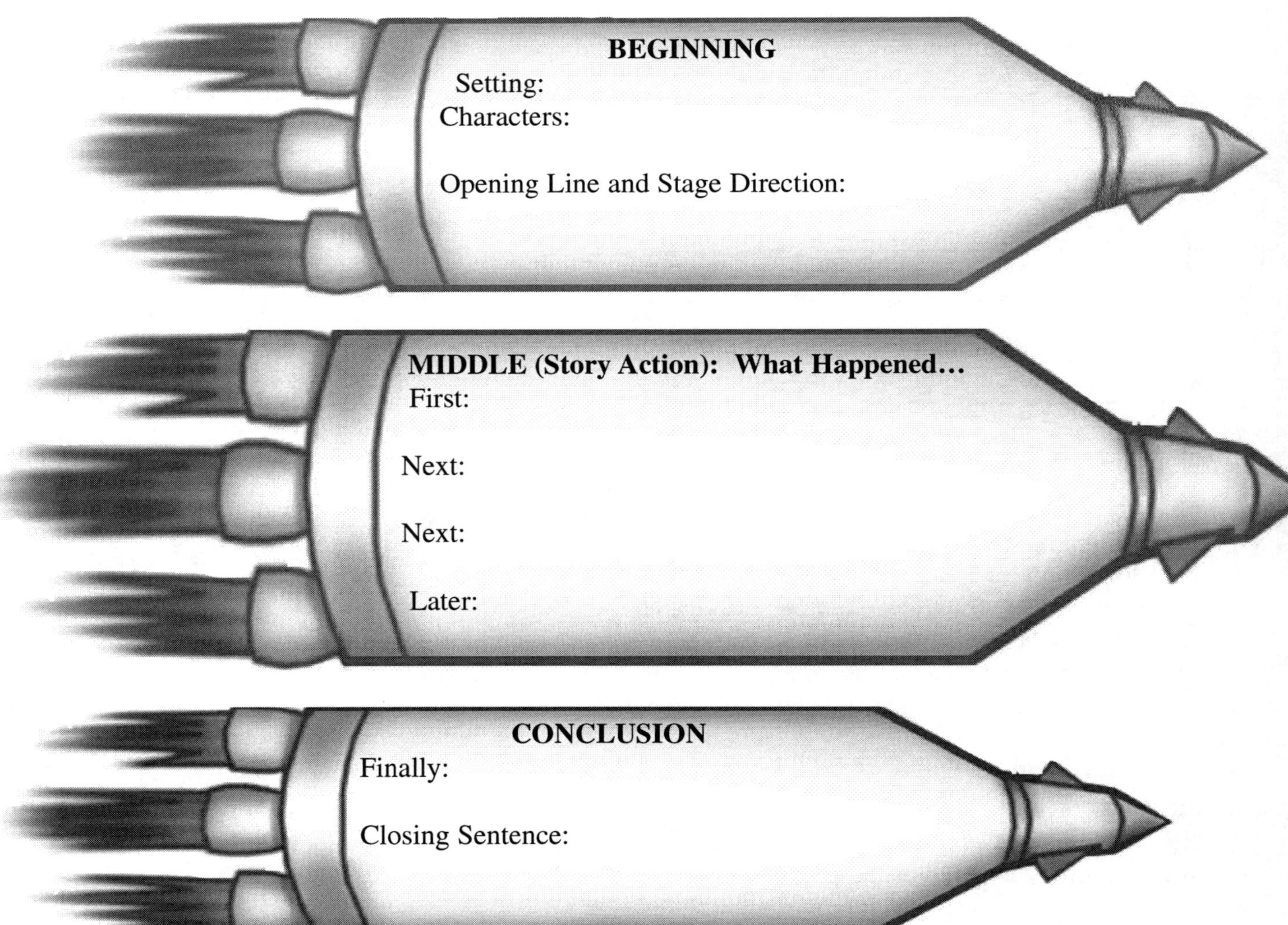

Science Fiction

COMPOSE

Remember to write your science-fiction story with a clear beginning, middle, and conclusion. Create interesting and expressive opening and closing sentences and strive for sentence and word variety. Don't forget to stay on topic as you write! Use details and dialogue to help your story develop fully. Relate the story events in the order that they occurred. Refer to your writing ideas from the pre-writing section to get started.

REVISE

Edit your science-fiction story by using the Writer's Checklist and the Editorial Symbols sheets. Then exchange papers with your pre-assigned writing partner. Each of you will use the same sheets to offer suggestions for improvement to the other. Now you are ready to rewrite your work in good form on another paper. Share the story with the whole class.

FOR MORE FUN

With a group of classmates design a city of the future. Each student will be responsible for a different segment of the city. Assign architecture, modes of transportation, clothing styles, governmental laws, classrooms, foods, etc., that might be part of a city in the next century. Display your projects in the school library.

All About Me

TOPIC
As a class assignment, you have been asked to write an autobiography. In it you must include the highlights of your life and your hopes for the future.

THINK ABOUT IT
Where and when were you born? Describe your family. Describe yourself. What are your earliest memories? Who were your earliest friends? What special adventures have you experienced in your life? What are your likes and dislikes? Successes and failures? Talents and interests? Where do you live now? Have you ever lived anywhere else? Who are your present friends? Where do you now attend school? Have you ever attended another school? Imagine the future and describe your plans for it.

GET ORGANIZED
Plan your autobiography. Start out with an effective opening sentence and describe the events of your life in the order that they happened. Add details to help the reader experience the story of your life. Include dialogue to make the characters in your writing come to life. Write a strong ending to your autobiography. Use the thought webs on this page to record your ideas.

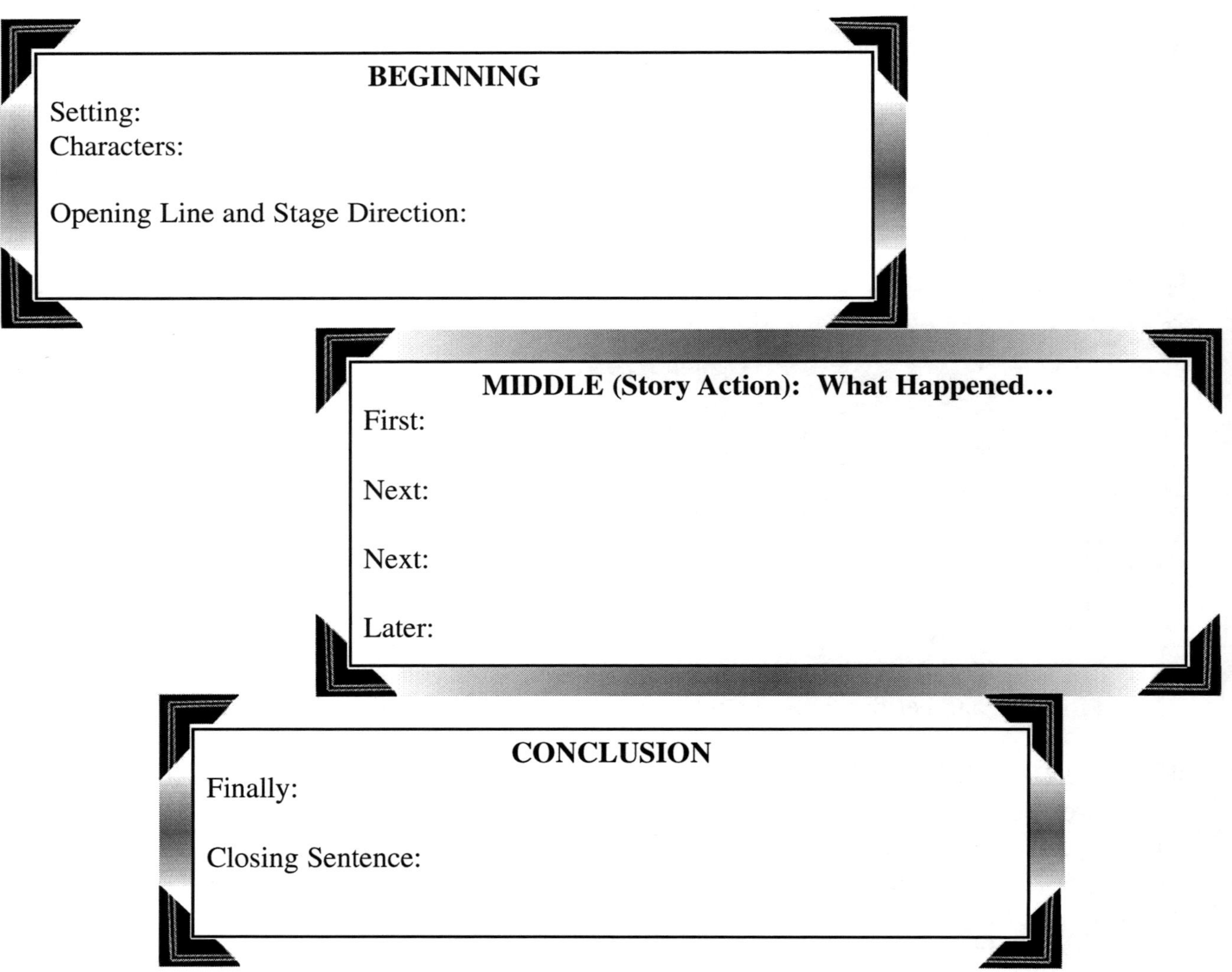

BEGINNING

Setting:

Characters:

Opening Line and Stage Direction:

MIDDLE (Story Action): What Happened…

First:

Next:

Next:

Later:

CONCLUSION

Finally:

Closing Sentence:

All About Me

COMPOSE

Remember to write your autobiography with a clear beginning, middle, and conclusion. Create interesting and expressive opening and closing sentences and strive for sentence and word variety. Don't forget to stay on topic as you write! Use details and dialogue to help your autobiography develop more fully. Relate the events of your life in the order that they occurred. Refer to your writing ideas from the pre-writing section to get started.

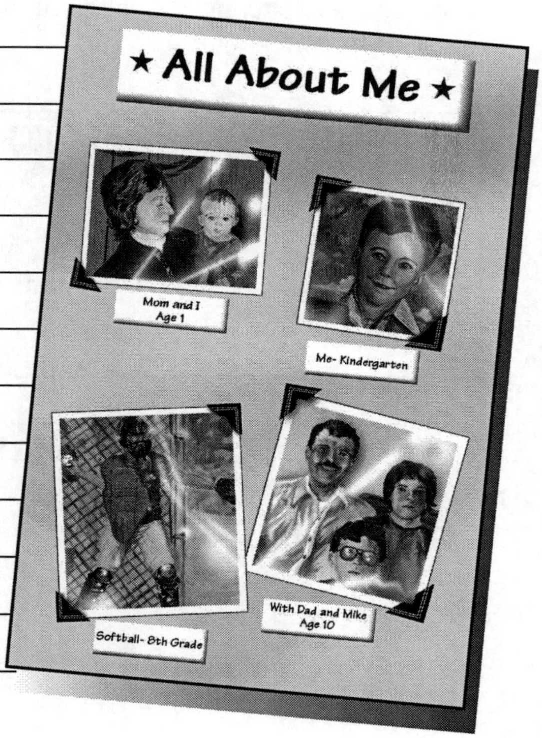

REVISE

Edit your autobiography by using the Writer's Checklist and the Editorial Symbols sheets. Then exchange papers with your pre-assigned writing partner. Each of you will use the same sheets to offer suggestions for improvement to the other. Now you are ready to rewrite your work in good form on another paper. Share your autobiography with the whole class.

FOR MORE FUN

Create an All About Me poster. Fill the poster with photos of special people, places, and things in your life. Include mementos that highlight the special times in your life as well as an illustration showing you in the future!

A Disappointment

TOPIC

Nearly everyone has endured a disappointment at one time or another. Recall an incident in which your expectations were not met. Tell how you responded to the disappointing situation.

THINK ABOUT IT

What were the circumstances of your disappointment? Where and when did the incident take place? Who else was involved in the situation? How did these people influence the outcome of the incident? Why were you so disappointed? What outcome would you have preferred? How did you react when you realized that your hopes would not be fulfilled? Do you wish you had reacted differently?

GET ORGANIZED

Plan your narrative writing. Start out with an effective opening sentence and describe the narrative events in the order that they happened. Add details to help the reader experience the story. Include dialogue to make the characters in your writing come to life. Write a strong ending to your narrative account. Use the thought webs on this page to record your ideas.

BEGINNING

Setting:
Characters:

Opening Line and Stage Direction:

MIDDLE (Story Action): What Happened…

First:

Next:

Next:

Later:

CONCLUSION

Finally:

Closing Sentence:

A Disappointment

COMPOSE

Remember to write your narrative story with a clear beginning, middle, and conclusion. Create interesting and expressive opening and closing sentences and strive for sentence and word variety. Don't forget to stay on topic as you write! Use details and dialogue to help your tale develop more fully. Relate the story events in the order that they occurred. Refer to your writing ideas from the pre-writing section to get started.

REVISE

Edit your narrative writing by using the Writer's Checklist and the Editorial Symbols sheets. Then exchange papers with your pre-assigned writing partner. Each of you will use the same sheets to offer suggestions for improvement to the other. Now you are ready to rewrite your work in good form on another paper. Share the story with the whole class.

FOR MORE FUN

Hold a class panel discussion to discuss the disappointing situation that you wrote about. Challenge classmates to brainstorm ways to change the situation so that you will enjoy a successful outcome the next time.

Headliners

TOPIC

You are a reporter for a local newspaper. Create a headline and a detailed supporting story for tomorrow's edition. A few possible headlines are the following: Community Bank Is Robbed, Unusual Traffic Jam Snarls Area Roadways, Surprise Snowfall Delights Children, and Local Team Wins Championship.

THINK ABOUT IT

What is your headline? Where and when does your story take place? Who are the people in your story? Are any animals involved in your story? Describe the story action. What obstacles confront the people in your story? How do they react to the story problems? Why is this an important story for your newspaper?

GET ORGANIZED

Plan your narrative writing. Start out with an effective opening sentence and describe the narrative events in the order that they happened. Don't forget that in a newspaper article you must be sure to include who, what, when, where, why, and how information. Add details to help the reader experience the story. Include dialogue to make the story come to life. Write a strong ending to your news story. Use the thought webs on this page to record your ideas.

BEGINNING

Headline:

Setting:

Characters:

Opening Sentence:

MIDDLE (Story Action): What Happened...

First:

Next:

Next:

Later:

CONCLUSION

Finally:

Closing Sentence:

Headliners

COMPOSE

Remember to write your news report with a clear beginning, middle, and conclusion. Create interesting and expressive opening and closing sentences and strive for sentence and word variety. Don't forget to stay on topic as you write! Use details and dialogue to help your story develop fully. Relate the story events in the order that they occurred. Refer to your writing ideas from the pre-writing section to get started.

REVISE

Edit your news report by using the Writer's Checklist and the Editorial Symbols sheets. Then exchange papers with your pre-assigned writing partner. Each of you will use the same sheets to offer suggestions for improvement to the other. Now you are ready to rewrite your work in good form on another paper. Share the news report with the whole class.

FOR MORE FUN

Create a class newspaper. Assemble all the news reports into one complete newspaper. Make "news photo" illustrations with captions underneath to enhance your articles.

Fable Fun

TOPIC

Fables are short tales that feature animals that possess human qualities. These stories usually conclude with a lesson, moral, or advice for the reader. *The Tortoise and the Hare* and *The Crow and the Pitcher* are familiar fables. Create an original fable in which an animal character learns a lesson.

THINK ABOUT IT

Who are your main characters? What qualities or character traits do they exhibit? If you choose Lion, the traits might be brave, strong, and king of the jungle. What moral will best suit the animal characters you have created? What are the main events of your fable? How are they sequenced? What are the animals' problems and concerns? Are their problems solved in a way that fits the moral of your story? HINT: You might want to think of the moral first.

GET ORGANIZED

Plan your fable. Start out with an effective opening sentence and describe the story events in the order that they happened. Add details to help the reader experience the story. Include dialogue to make the characters in your writing come to life. Write a strong ending to your fable. Use the thought webs on this page to record your ideas.

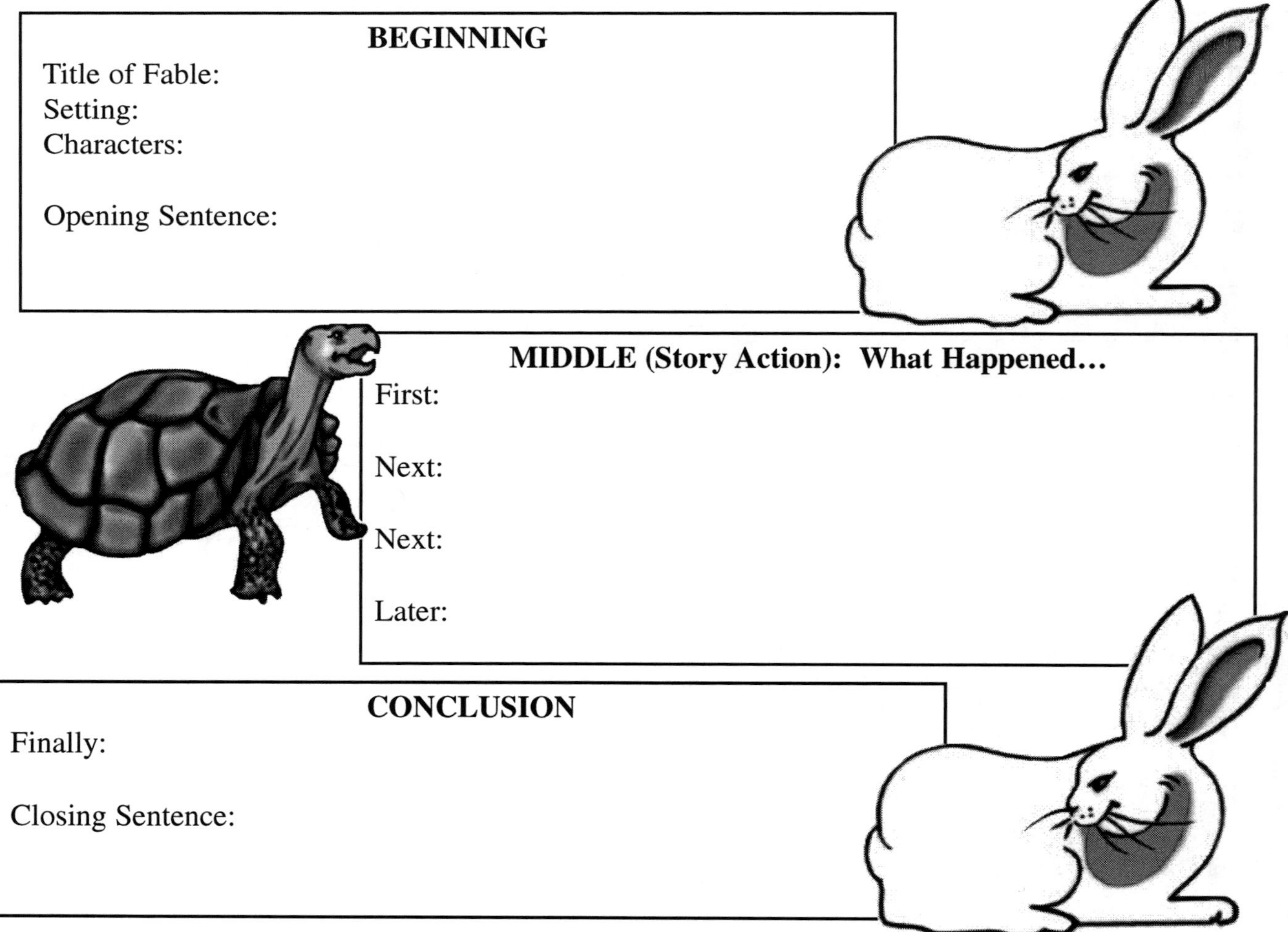

BEGINNING

Title of Fable:
Setting:
Characters:

Opening Sentence:

MIDDLE (Story Action): What Happened…

First:

Next:

Next:

Later:

CONCLUSION

Finally:

Closing Sentence:

Fable Fun

COMPOSE

Remember to write your fable with a clear beginning, middle, and conclusion. Create interesting and expressive opening and closing sentences and strive for sentence and word variety. Don't forget to stay on topic as you write! Use details and dialogue to help your fable develop fully. Relate the story events in the order that they occurred. Refer to your writing ideas from the pre-writing section to get started.

REVISE

Edit your fable by using the Writer's Checklist and the Editorial Symbols sheets. Then exchange papers with your pre-assigned writing partner. Each of you will use the same sheets to offer suggestions for improvement to the other. Now you are ready to rewrite your work in good form on another paper. Share the fable with the whole class.

FOR MORE FUN

Create a mural of all the animal characters in the fables. Display it on a hall bulletin board.

For the Very First Time

TOPIC

Describe an occasion in your life when you did something special for the first time. Perhaps you took an airplane trip, learned to ride a bicycle, or stayed home alone. Write an essay about this "first" experience.

THINK ABOUT IT

Where and when did your first experience take place? Who else was part of it? How did these people help or hinder you? What part of the experience was a first for you? How did you feel at the beginning? What problems did you have to overcome as the experience developed? Were you proud of your accomplishment at the end of the experience? Why?

GET ORGANIZED

Plan your narrative writing. Start out with an effective opening sentence and describe the story events in the order that they happened. Add details to help the reader experience the story. Include dialogue to make the characters in your writing come to life. Write a strong ending to your narrative account. Use the thought webs on this page to record your ideas.

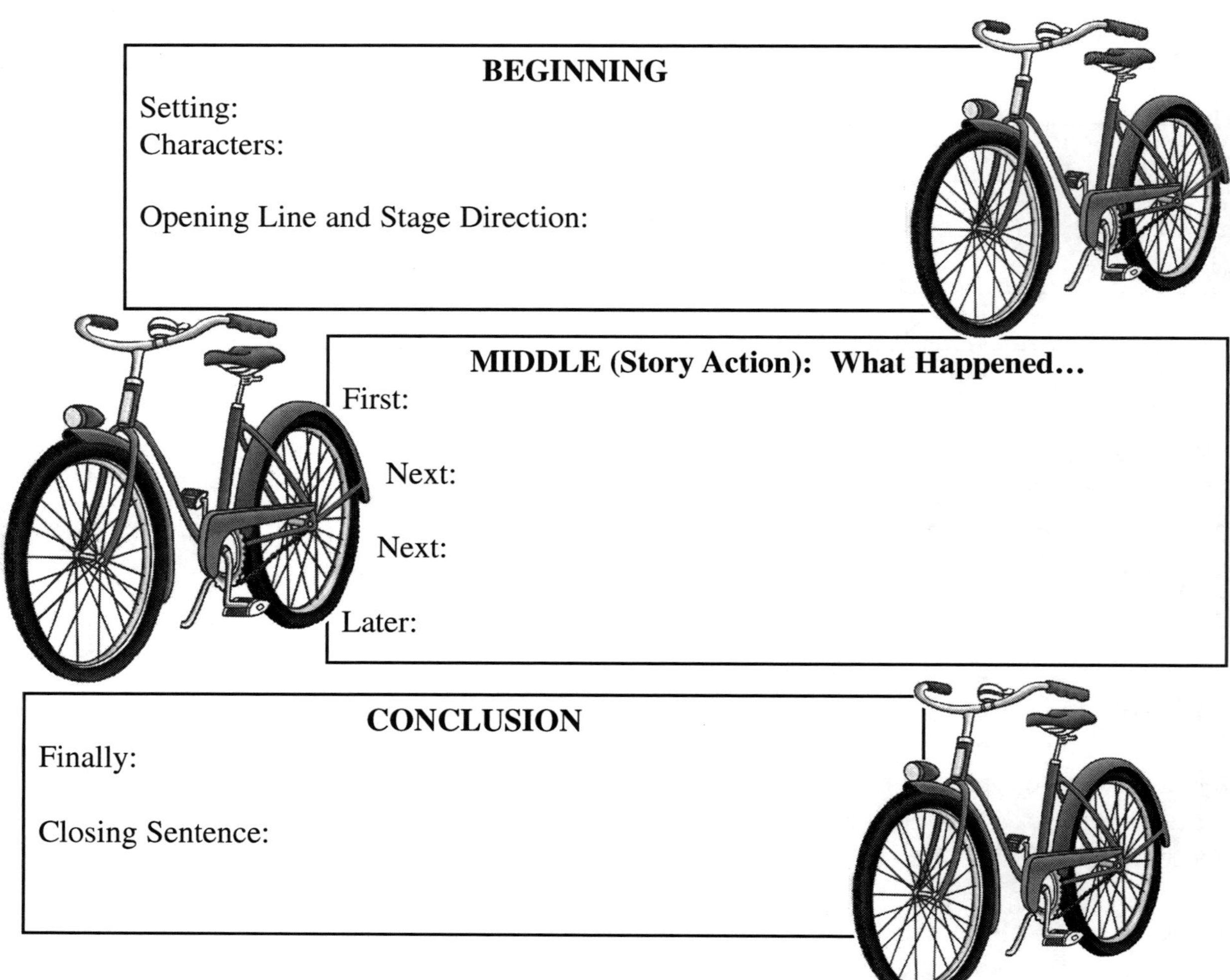

BEGINNING

Setting:

Characters:

Opening Line and Stage Direction:

MIDDLE (Story Action): What Happened…

First:

Next:

Next:

Later:

CONCLUSION

Finally:

Closing Sentence:

For the Very First Time

COMPOSE

Remember to write your narrative essay with a clear beginning, middle, and conclusion. Create interesting and expressive opening and closing sentences and strive for sentence and word variety. Don't forget to stay on topic as you write! Use details and dialogue to help your essay develop fully. Relate the story events in the order that they occurred. Refer to your writing ideas from the pre-writing section to get started.

REVISE

Edit your essay by using the Writer's Checklist and the Editorial Symbols sheets. Then exchange papers with your pre-assigned writing partner. Each of you will use the same sheets to offer suggestions for improvement to the other. Now you are ready to rewrite your work in good form on another paper. Share the story with the whole class.

FOR MORE FUN

Pretend that you are a TV reporter who has been assigned to cover breaking news. (The breaking news is your "first" experience.) Describe the experience to your audience as an eyewitness news reporter would.

Narrative Poetry

TOPIC

A narrative poem tells a story. Rhyming patterns vary with the poem. Some well-known narrative poems include *Paul Revere's Ride* and *Hiawatha's Childhood,* by Henry Wadsworth Longfellow; *Lincoln* and *Washington,* by Nancy Byrd Turner; and *Columbus,* by Joaquin Miller. Create an original narrative poem about the life of a famous person. Before you start, read some narrative poems and gather biographical information about the subject of your poem.

THINK ABOUT IT

Why is your subject famous? Which part of the person's life will you highlight in your poem? Who else will be mentioned? What is the setting? Which historical facts will you include? How did the subject finally overcome obstacles to achieve his or her goal? What type of rhyming pattern will best suit your poem? What techniques will you use to make your narrative sound more poetic? Alliteration, similes, metaphors, personification, and repetition are some choices.

GET ORGANIZED

Plan your narrative poem. Start out with an effective opening line and describe the story events in the order that they happened. Add details to help the reader experience the story. Use colorful and descriptive words and try to include poetic techniques. Narrative poems often include dialogue to make the characters come to life. Write a strong ending to your poem. Use the thought webs on this page to record your ideas.

BEGINNING

Title (Famous Person):
Setting:
Characters:

Opening Line:

MIDDLE (Story Action): What Happened…

First:

Next:

Next:

Later:

CONCLUSION

Finally:

Closing Sentence:

Narrative Poetry

COMPOSE

Remember to write your narrative poem with a clear beginning, middle, and conclusion. Create interesting and expressive opening and closing lines and strive for sentence and word variety. Don't forget to stay on topic as you write your poem! Use details and dialogue to help your poem develop fully. Relate the narrative events in the order that they occurred. Include lots of poetic language. Refer to your writing ideas from the pre-writing section to get started.

REVISE

Edit your narrative poem by using the Writer's Checklist and the Editorial Symbols sheets. Then exchange papers with your pre-assigned writing partner. Each of you will use the same sheets to offer suggestions for improvement to the other. Now you are ready to rewrite your work in good form on another paper. Share the poem with the whole class.

FOR MORE FUN

A ballad is a narrative poem that is set to music. Create original music for your narrative poem or set the words to a familiar tune. Perform your ballad for your classmates.

A Person in My Life

TOPIC

Our lives are often touched and influenced by other people. Write an essay about a special person who has been supportive and encouraging and who has been a positive role model for you.

THINK ABOUT IT

Who is the special person? How long have you known him or her? How and when did you meet? Describe the person. Give examples of his or her personality traits and qualities to admire. Recall several experiences that you shared with this person. In what ways has he or she influenced your life?

GET ORGANIZED

Plan your narrative writing. Start out with an effective opening sentence and describe the narrative events in the order that they happened. Add details to help the reader experience the story. Include dialogue to make the characters in your writing come to life. Write a strong ending to your essay. Use the thought webs on this page to record your ideas for your narrative writing.

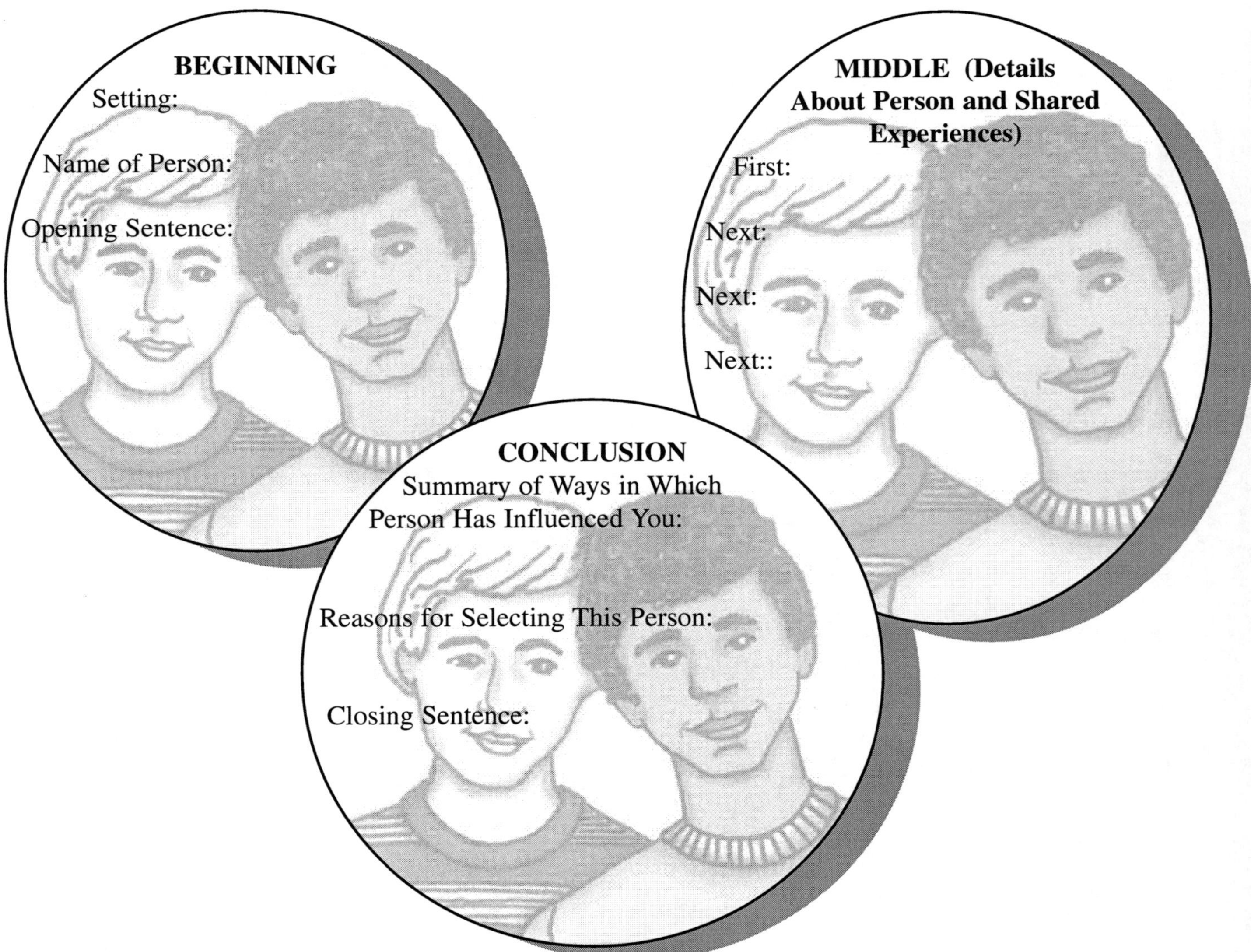

A Person in My Life

COMPOSE

Remember to write your narrative essay with a clear beginning, middle, and conclusion. Create interesting and expressive opening and closing sentences and strive for sentence and word variety. Don't forget to stay on topic as you write! Use details and dialogue to help your essay develop fully. Relate the story events in the order that they occurred. Refer to your writing ideas from the pre-writing section to get started.

REVISE

Edit your narrative writing by using the Writer's Checklist and the Editorial Symbols sheets. Then exchange papers with your pre-assigned writing partner. Each of you will use the same sheets to offer suggestions for improvement to the other. Now you are ready to rewrite your work in good form on another paper. Share the essay with the whole class.

FOR MORE FUN

Using colored construction paper or poster board, design and cut out a large, key-shaped pattern. Paste the good copy of your essay on it. After sharing the class essays orally, hang them on a class bulletin board. Send a copy of the essay to the key person with an extra note of thanks.

Tell a Tall Tale

TOPIC

You've probably read one or more tall tales. Paul Bunyan, Mike Fink, and John Henry are some tall-tale heroes who are larger-than-life figures. These literary wonders can easily complete breathtaking deeds. Now it is your chance to create your own tall tale with a hero equal to those you have read about.

THINK ABOUT IT

What is your hero's name? In what ways is he or she an exaggerated figure? Appearance? Abilities? Deeds? Decide on a setting for your story. How many other characters are involved in the story? What gigantic problems will your hero be challenged to solve? How will these feats be accomplished? In what ways are your hero's adventures humorous?

GET ORGANIZED

Plan your narrative writing. Start out with an effective opening sentence and describe the narrative events in the order that they happened. Add details to help the reader experience the story. Include dialogue to make the characters in your writing come to life. Write a strong ending to your tall tale. Use the thought webs on this page to record your ideas.

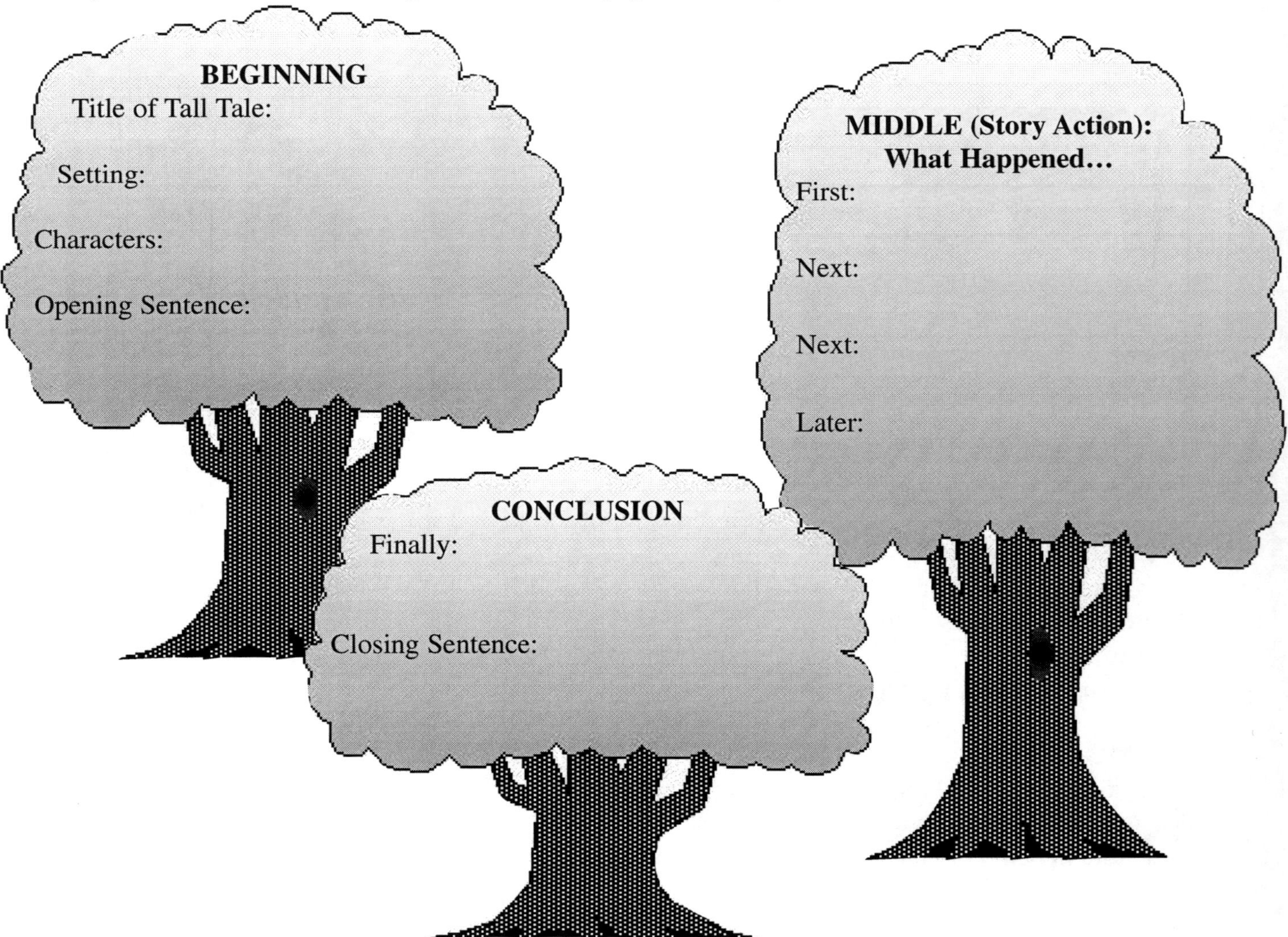

Tell a Tall Tale

COMPOSE

Remember to write your tall tale with a clear beginning, middle, and conclusion. Create interesting and expressive opening and closing sentences and strive for sentence and word variety. Don't forget to stay on topic as you write! Use details and dialogue to help your tale develop more fully. Relate the story events in the order that they occurred. Refer to your writing ideas from the pre-writing section to get started.

REVISE

Edit your tall tale by using the Writer's Checklist and the Editorial Symbols sheets. Then exchange papers with your pre-assigned writing partner. Each of you will use the same sheets to offer suggestions for improvement to the other. Now you are ready to rewrite your work in good form on another paper. Share the story with the whole class.

FOR MORE FUN

Create a comic strip with your tall-tale hero as the central character. Read the comic strip to younger students.

Time of Your Life

TOPIC

Have you ever wanted to be older or younger than you are now? Imagine that you are a different age. Write an essay that tells how your life would be changed.

THINK ABOUT IT

What age would you choose to be? Imagine how you would look and act at this age? In what ways would your life be different? What new responsibilities would you have? Imagine a specific experience that you might have at this age: driving a car, getting married, going to college, etc. In what ways would people react differently to you at the new age? Why would you rather be this age than your real age?

GET ORGANIZED

Plan your narrative essay. Start out with an effective opening sentence and describe the narrative events in the order that they happened. Add details to help the reader experience the story. Include dialogue to make the characters in your writing come to life. Write a strong ending to your narrative writing. Use the thought webs on this page to record your ideas.

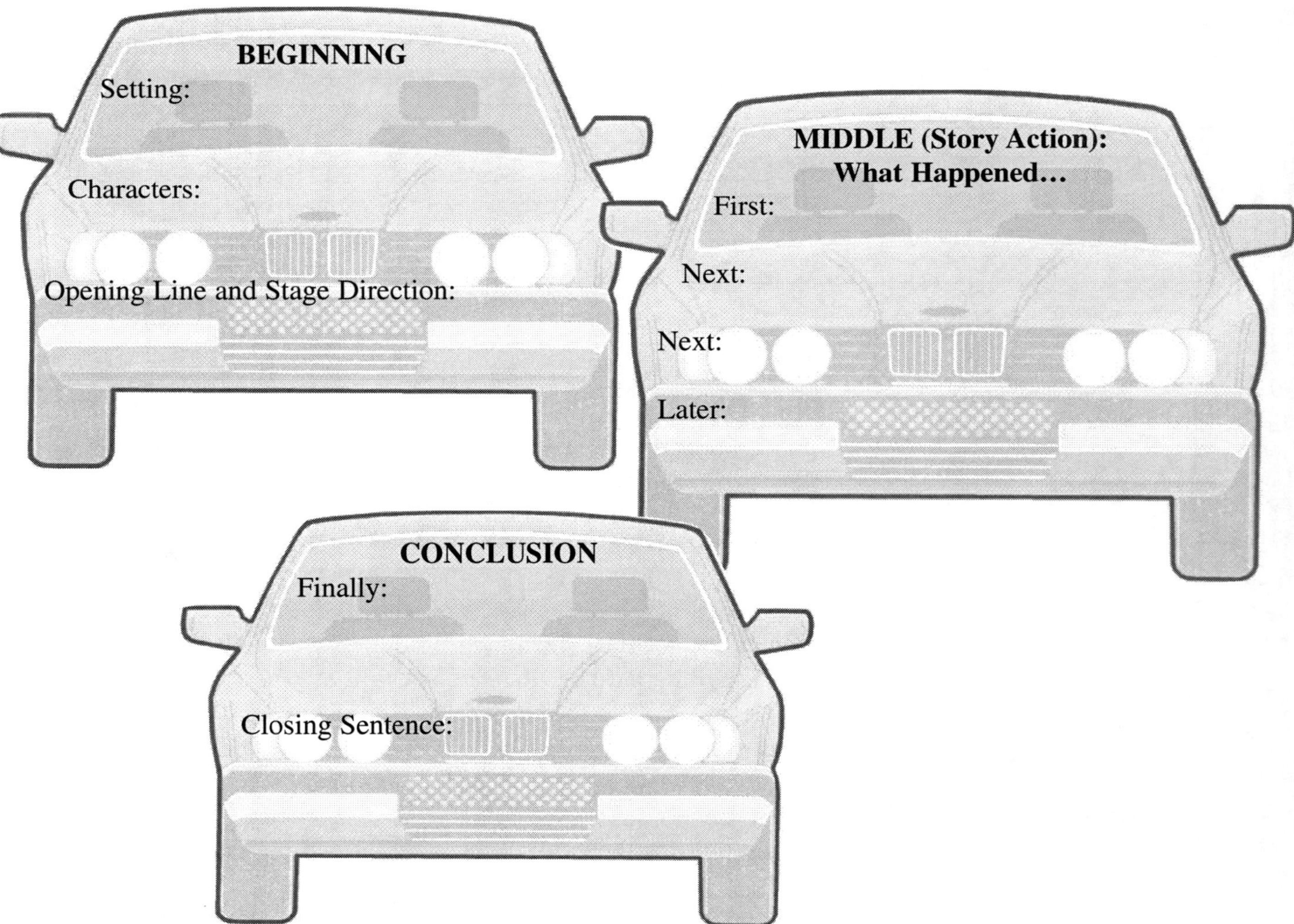

Time of Your Life

COMPOSE

Remember to write your narrative essay with a clear beginning, middle, and conclusion. Create interesting and expressive opening and closing sentences and strive for sentence and word variety. Don't forget to stay on topic as you write! Use details and dialogue to help your essay develop fully. Relate the story events in the order that they occurred. Refer to your writing ideas from the pre-writing section to get started.

REVISE

Edit your essay by using the Writer's Checklist and the Editorial Symbols sheets. Then exchange papers with your pre-assigned writing partner. Each of you will use the same sheets to offer suggestions for improvement to the other. Now you are ready to rewrite your work in good form on another paper. Share the story with the whole class.

FOR MORE FUN

Create a project cube by covering a square paper box with construction paper. Design pictures of yourself at your chosen age and attach them to the cube.

The Story Behind the Picture

TOPIC
The picture on the right is the story prompt for this writing activity. Use your imagination to create an exciting story based on the illustration.

THINK ABOUT IT
What is happening? Are things as they seem?
Who are the main and supporting characters?
What caused the situation? Is anyone in danger?
How will the problem be solved?
What lessons are learned?

GET ORGANIZED
Plan your narrative writing. Start out with an effective opening sentence and describe the narrative events in the order that they happened. Add details to help the reader experience the story. Include dialogue to make the characters in your writing come to life. Write a strong ending to your narrative account. Use the thought webs on this page to record your ideas.

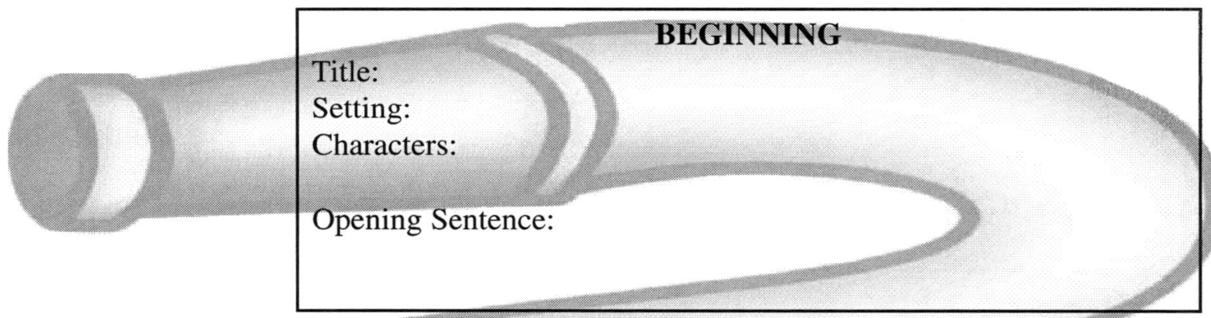

BEGINNING

Title:
Setting:
Characters:

Opening Sentence:

MIDDLE (Story Action): What Happened…

First:

Next:

Next:

Later:

CONCLUSION

Finally:

Closing Sentence:

The Story Behind the Picture

COMPOSE

Remember to write your narrative story with a clear beginning, middle, and conclusion. Create interesting and expressive opening and closing sentences and strive for sentence and word variety. Don't forget to stay on topic as you write! Use details and dialogue to help your story develop fully. Relate the story events in the order that they occurred. Refer to your writing ideas from the pre-writing section to get started.

REVISE

Edit your story by using the Writer's Checklist and the Editorial Symbols sheets. Then exchange papers with your pre-assigned writing partner. Each of you will use the same sheets to offer suggestions for improvement to the other. Now you are ready to rewrite your work in good form on another paper. Share the story with the whole class.

FOR MORE FUN

Make a class collage of newspaper articles that feature local heroes and their deeds. Invite those heroes to your classroom to speak about their experience.

Holiday Memories

TOPIC
Holidays are special times. Recall a favorite holiday celebration that you enjoyed and write a story telling why it was so memorable.

THINK ABOUT IT
What was the holiday? Where and when did you celebrate it? Who were the people who shared the celebration with you? What happened at this holiday that made it so unforgettable? Why are holiday celebrations important?

GET ORGANIZED
Plan your narrative writing. Start out with an effective opening sentence and describe the narrative events in the order that they happened. Add details to help the reader experience the story. Include dialogue to make the characters in your writing come to life. Write a strong ending to your narrative account. Use the thought webs on this page to record your ideas.

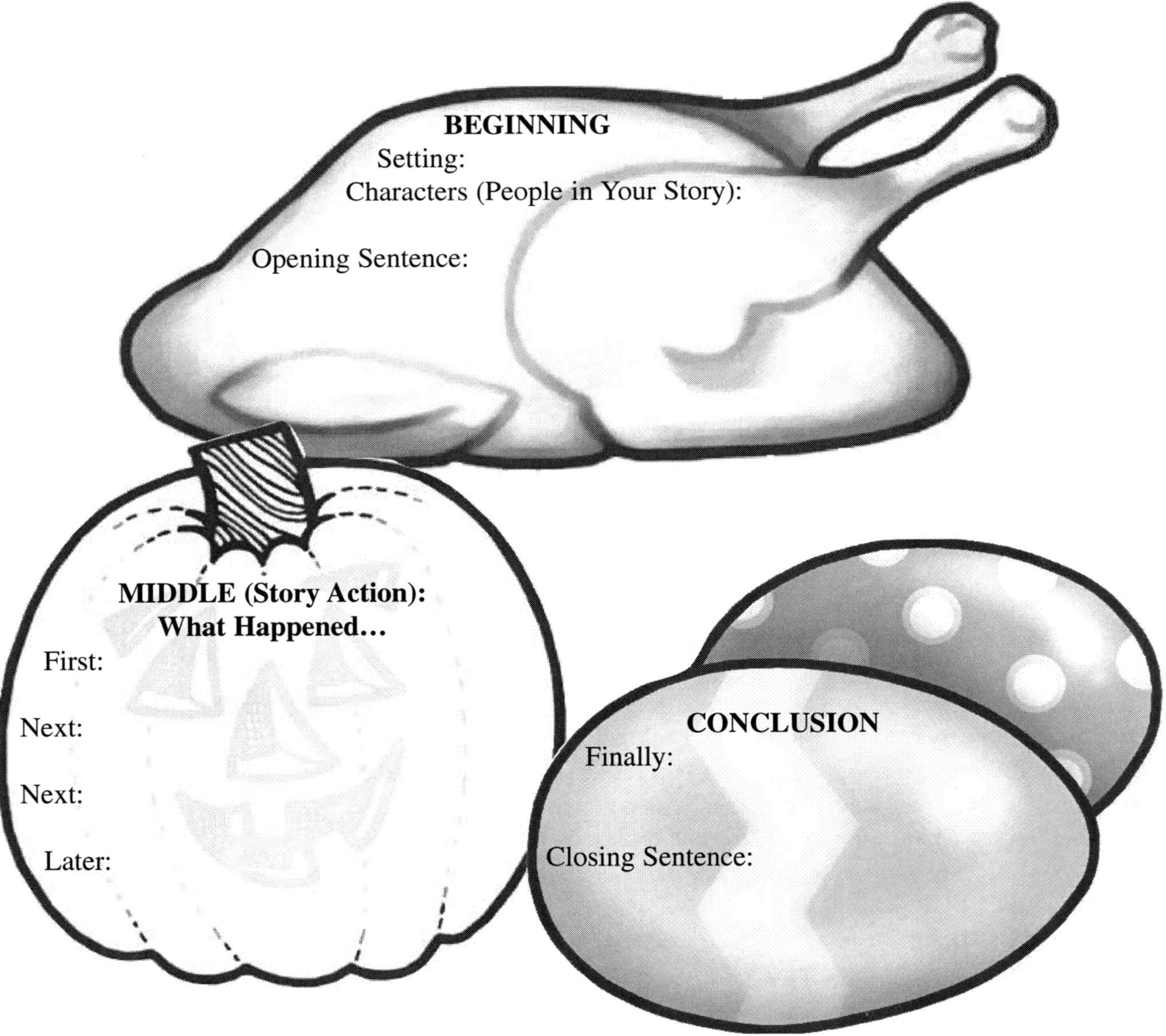

Holiday Memories

COMPOSE

Remember to write your narrative story with a clear beginning, middle, and conclusion. Create interesting and expressive opening and closing sentences and strive for sentence and word variety. Don't forget to stay on topic as you write! Use details and dialogue to help your story develop fully. Relate the story events in the order that they occurred. Refer to your writing ideas from the pre-writing section to get started.

REVISE

Edit your story by using the Writer's Checklist and the Editorial Symbols sheets. Then exchange papers with your pre-assigned writing partner. Each of you will use the same sheets to offer suggestions for improvement to the other. Now you are ready to rewrite your work in good form on another paper. Share the story with the whole class.

FOR MORE FUN

Create a greeting card for the holiday you described in your story. Write a poem that describes your feelings about the holiday celebration. Attach the poem to the inside of your card.

Additional Topic Ideas for Narrative Writing

1. Imagine that you are an inventor on the brink of a new discovery. Describe your invention and tell how it will benefit society.

2. Think of a difficult decision that you were forced to make. Tell about the situation that led to the decision. How did you feel after the decision was made?

3. Write a new ending to a favorite story.

4. Imagine that you own a time machine that can travel backward or forward in time. Decide whether to travel back in time to witness a historical event or to set the machine ahead to visit the world of the future. Write about your adventure.

5. You have just completed your first week at a new school. Write a letter to friends in your old community telling about your new experience.

6. Write a scary story. Set a scary scene and use vivid vocabulary that will add to the mood of your tale.

7. Write about a wish or a dream that you hope will come true someday. What steps are you taking to make it a reality?

8. You have always been a fan of mystery stories. Now it is your turn to write your own. Think of clues that will lead the central character to the right conclusion. Make your story a suspenseful one.

9. Have you ever been treated unfairly? Write about the incident and tell if the problem was ever corrected to your satisfaction.

10. You are spending vacation time with relatives in another country. Write a diary entry telling about your day's activities.